125
Animals That Changed the World

125 Animals That Changed the World

INSPIRING TALES OF FURRY FRIENDS & FOUR-LEGGED HEROES, PLUS MORE AMAZING ANIMAL ANTICS!

The Sawtooth
Pack Page 83

NATIONAL
GEOGRAPHIC
KiDS

WASHINGTON, D.C.

Contents

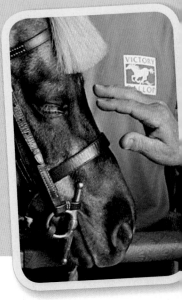

Introduction

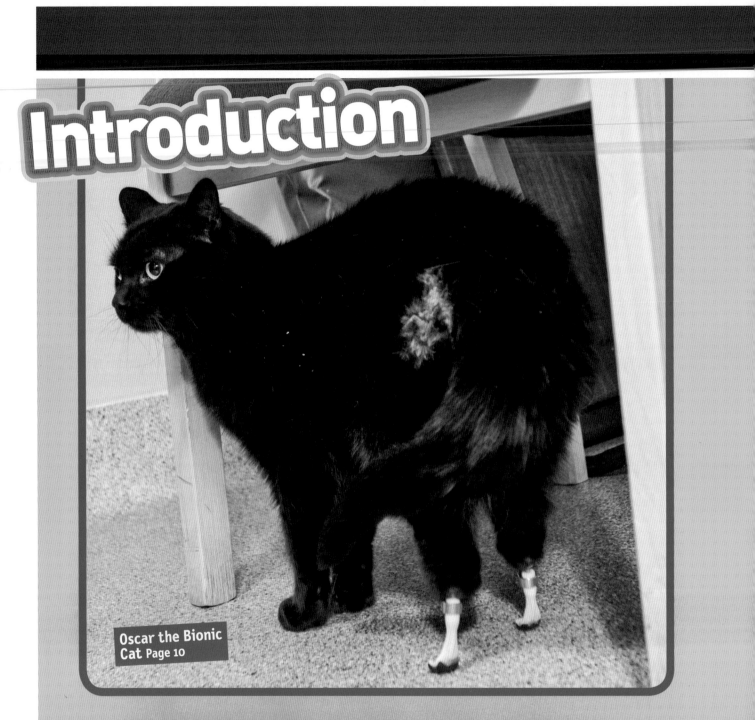

Oscar the Bionic
Cat Page 10

A bionic cat. A parrot who saved a baby's life. Quails born in space. Dolphin soldiers. There are so many amazing animals on our planet, but some have stories so astounding that they affected us, and even the world, **in a big way.**

This book is packed with important creatures that accomplished great things during their lifetimes—monkeys, dogs, cats, horses, birds, bears, turtles, elephants, and even jellyfish. Each has a unique story, but the one thing they have in common is that they all made significant contributions to humankind: They changed the world.

Some of these animals advanced our understanding of science or medicine; others showed great heroism or taught us about our own humanity. Some gave willingly. Others were "recruited," sparking debates over whether the benefits outweigh the cost of involving animals without their consent. But for good or for ill, all changed our world—in big and small ways.

Changing the world sounds like a pretty tall order, but it might not be as tall as you think. Big changes are not always about doing big things. A small act can have a lasting impact. Some of these animals may have only changed the life of *one* person. Others "changed the world" by bringing joy or hope to a select few. And some inspired changes that affected the entire planet. But every action, even a tiny one, is like a drop that creates a ripple in a pond. It may spread far and wide or inspire others to act as well.

We owe these animals a great debt—not only did they make our lives better through their services, but they also continue to teach us an important lesson: Everyone, whether on two legs or four, whether small or big, can change the world—including you!

Ready for Takeoff!
Page 77

Buttercup: Super Sloth Page 26

An Artist's Touch
Page 99

OSCAR
THE BIONIC CAT

Oscar was living a comfortable life on Jersey, the largest of the Channel Islands, between England and France. One day, he chose to nap in the sun. Yet the field he chose for a snooze wasn't a safe place. Oscar was struck by a piece of farm equipment and his legs were badly hurt. But veterinary surgeon Noel Fitzpatrick didn't want to give up on this young, healthy cat. Instead, he wanted to give Oscar a new pair of bionic back legs: electronic legs that he and his colleagues would create themselves. It took a long surgery, but the doctors successfully attached the new limbs. Oscar slowly healed until the new legs became part of his body. This wonder kitty had become the world's first cat with two bionic legs! Robo-kitty Oscar took to his new legs right away and now enjoys roaming around. Dr. Fitzpatrick and his vet team hope that the things they learned during Oscar's treatment might one day help humans who need new limbs.

Oscar holds two world records: one for being the first animal with two bionic leg implants, and the other for being the first animal to receive implants in moving joints.

OSCAR

SERGEANT STUBBY

Stubby served in the trenches in France for 18 months and participated in 17 battles.

When Stubby joined the 102nd Infantry Regiment during World War I, he was supposed to be a *mascot*. Dogs were against regulations, but Stubby was smuggled into camp. After being discovered, he got to stay because he boosted the men's spirits. Stubby was a good soldier, joining in drills and howling along with bugle calls. He even learned to salute by raising his paw! And on the battlefields of France, he excelled at locating lost or wounded soldiers and leading rescuers back to them. He once caught a German soldier by the seat of his pants, holding him until American soldiers found him. Stubby's greatest contribution might have been his keen hearing—because he could hear the whine of incoming shells before anyone else, the men learned to duck when he ducked. When the war ended, Stubby went back to America, but he continued serving. He helped sell victory war bonds and marched in parades. He even became the mascot of Yale University's football team!

STUBBY

HUBERTA THE HIKING HIPPO

At first, everyone thought Huberta was male, and they called her Hubert!

No one knew why Huberta started walking. No one thought to ask her. If they had, she wouldn't have answered. Huberta was a hippopotamus—and as everyone knows, hippos aren't big talkers! Huberta left her watering hole in South Africa one day in 1928 and continued walking south for the next three years. As she ambled along, Huberta passed through many villages. She often surprised farmers in their fields. As she nibbled her way through cabbage and sugarcane, Huberta became well known. Newspapers from all over the world followed her adventures. Some people even tried to catch her to take her to a zoo, but Huberta had other plans: She wanted to keep walking! She avoided capture again and again. Nothing could stop her! Many people were inspired by her solo stroll. During the 1930s, South Africa was experiencing a depression, and people needed a symbol of hope. Huberta the unstoppable hippo fit the bill! In the end, Huberta covered more than 1,000 miles (1,609 km) ... and became a national icon to boot.

THESE FEET WERE MADE FOR WALKIN'!

HUBERTA WAS A HIPPOPOTAMUS LIKE THE ONE PICTURED HERE.

THE TRACKING TRIO

Didi, Bonnie, and Clyde might be small compared to the animals they protect, but no job is too big for this trio of trackers. Trained by Big Life Foundation, the daring dogs sniff out poachers—people who hunt protected animals like elephants and rhinoceroses—in Kenya and Tanzania. Although it can be impossible for humans to find poachers who have committed crimes, it's all in a day's work for tracker dogs, who can lead their handlers right to a poacher's door! The heroic hounds have even sniffed out weapons and traps before poachers could use them, saving countless animals. In fact, Didi, Bonnie, and Clyde are so good at their jobs that they have started to deter poachers from hunting at all; the poachers know that they can't escape the power of a tracker dog's nose. Protecting wildlife is a big job, but it's no match for these big heroes!

BONNIE

CLYDE

DIDI

SMOKEY BEAR

SMOKEY

SMOKEY

SMOKEY

Firefighters were struggling to contain two blazes near New Mexico's Lincoln National Forest in May 1950. Then something dangerous happened. A swift wind of 70 miles an hour (113 km/h) pushed the flames, catching about 30 men in the fire's path. Their only hope was to lie facedown on a rockslide and wait for the fire to roar past them. The men survived unharmed! Nearby, a tiny black bear cub had not fared as well. Firefighters found the singed cub clinging to the side of a charred pine tree. His paws were badly burned, and he was scared. The firefighters rescued him and treated his injuries. Little Smokey made a full recovery, became an important mascot to the U.S. Forest Service, and spent his life at the National Zoo in Washington, D.C., as a "spokesbear" for fire safety. Soon, he had inspired a cartoon bear who successfully taught kids and adults across the United States how to help prevent forest fires. To this day, the cub—and his message of fire safety—live on in Smokey Bear!

Today, Smokey also teaches about prescribed fires—controlled burns that help maintain healthy ecosystems.

BEAUTY,
BIONIC EAGLE

Beauty was hunting for prey in the mountains of Alaska, U.S.A., when it happened. There was a loud crack. A hunter's bullet shattered the bald eagle's beak. She fell to the ground and lay there for days. Luckily, a policeman discovered her and rushed her to a wildlife center. There, her slow journey toward recovery began. After many months, Beauty was stronger, but her beak was so badly damaged she couldn't eat or drink without human help. A wildlife rehabilitator and an engineer came up with a crazy idea: They would make Beauty a *new* beak, built from a 3D printer. No one knew if it would work. But when the beak was built—at last!—Beauty could eat and drink on her own again. Over time, her broken beak began regrowing. She needed her new beak less and less. Her story inspired scientists to consider this technology to treat injured birds and other animals, and they learned about the power of healing along the way.

BEAUTY

MONTAUCIEL
THE FLYING SHEEP

A duck, a rooster, and a sheep got into a hot air balloon ... It sounds like the start of a joke, but this was no laughing matter. *This* was science! The year was 1783, and the king and queen of France had been invited to witness a spectacle. Two brothers were unveiling their new invention, a hot air balloon. It was a machine that would not only fly, but carry passengers as well! The duck was the "control" of the experiment—everyone knew ducks could fly, so they were certain the feathered passenger would survive a flight at high heights. The rooster wasn't much of a flier, but he was still a *bird*. All eyes were on the sheep, named Montauciel. If a sheep could survive the flight, then humans might be next! The roar of a cannon marked the balloon's liftoff. The audience eagerly watched as it rose and drifted for nearly two miles (3 km). When it landed safely, Montauciel climbed out of the basket and began nibbling on grass. He was apparently no worse for wear after his historic eight-minute flight. Nor did he realize that he had just paved the way for human aviation! Two months after Montauciel's riveting ride, two humans flew in the world's first untethered hot air balloon ride.

MONTAUCIEL WAS A SHEEP LIKE THE ONE SEEN HERE.

Montauciel means "flying up to the sky" in French.

CASPER THE COMMUTING CAT

CASPER

Like a lot of cat owners, Sue Finden wondered where her pet, Casper, disappeared to every day. Unlike most cats, though, it turned out Casper was a regular rider on the local bus. He showed up at the stop near his home in England like clockwork, and all the drivers knew him. He took the number 3 bus every day, riding the entirety of an 11-mile (18-km) route. Sometimes Casper looked out the window; sometimes he curled up in a purring ball and went to sleep. At the end of the loop, drivers always let Casper off at the correct stop. No one really knew why he made the trip each day, but then again, no one bothered to ask! Casper's presence on the bus certainly cheered his fellow passengers. Eventually, news of his bus-riding ways made the papers and cheered people across the globe, too!

BINTI-JUA: A MOTHER'S LOVE

No one saw the three-year-old boy climbing the fence at the Brookfield Zoo near Chicago, Illinois. But when he fell more than 15 feet (4.6 m) into the gorilla enclosure, everyone noticed. Inside the enclosure were seven gorillas, including Binti-Jua. Binti-Jua was a mother herself. She knew that the gorilla enclosure was not a good place for a human boy. And so, with her own infant clinging to her back, this western lowland gorilla moved slowly toward him. The boy's mother and the stunned spectators had no idea what would happen next—would she harm him? But when Binti-Jua reached the boy, she carefully lifted him up and cradled him in her arms. She turned her back to the other gorillas to shield the boy. Then Binti-Jua heard the door to the enclosure open. She carried the boy to the doorway and laid him gently at the feet of waiting paramedics. The boy made a full recovery. Binti-Jua did what any mother would do: protect, comfort, and help.

BINTI-JUA

Binti-Jua means "daughter of sunshine" in Swahili.

BUCEPHALUS

THE TAMING OF
BUCEPHALUS

Years before Alexander the Great became a powerful Macedonian king in 336 B.C.E., he was a teenager with a problem. Alexander's father had been given a horse that no one could tame. Alexander watched as the king and many others tried. The horse seemed wild and vicious. But to Alexander, it seemed like something else: scared. Alexander thought the horse was afraid of its shadow. He asked his father if *he* could try to tame the horse. Everyone laughed. What chance did a boy have against this savage animal? But Alexander was determined. He took the horse by its bridle and turned it to face the sun so their shadows were behind them. Miraculously, the horse began to calm down and Alexander gently climbed onto its back. From that moment on, Bucephalus would accept no other rider but Alexander. The two rode into battle together, conquering lands and creating an empire that ranged from Egypt into what is now India— the largest the world had ever seen. The pair changed the face of the world and forever altered history by establishing cities and uniting nations. Both rider and horse remain legendary to this day, thousands of years later.

MERCURY

Wartime pigeons flew through hails of bullets, in bad weather, or with injuries. Many didn't survive ... but Mercury was different. Selected to work for Danish resistance fighters during World War II, Mercury and 11 other pigeons were smuggled into Denmark. They would relay information about German military strength. The mission was vital—so much so that all 12 resistance birds were released carrying the same information. The pigeons had to fly 1,520 miles (2,446 km) back home to England carrying the intelligence. They faced countless risks, including being shot or attacked by predators, collapsing into the sea from exhaustion, or simply getting lost. As the handlers waited for the pigeons to return, they grew anxious. There was no sign of the birds; the task had been too much for them. All of them, that is, but one: Mercury alone completed the mission, delivering crucial intelligence and contributing to the Allied war effort.

PEP

Al Capone, the infamous gangster, served time in the same prison as Pep!

PRISON DOG PEP

It was 1924 and someone new had arrived at Eastern State Penitentiary, a prison in Pennsylvania, U.S.A. He was known to some as Pep the Black, and to others as Prisoner C2559. But no matter what you called him, Pep was innocent. Oh, and he was also a dog! Pep had been the dog of the governor of Pennsylvania, living in the lap of luxury. That is, until he decided to chew up the governor's sofa cushions. Chewing cushions isn't exactly a *crime*, but the governor's wife wouldn't have it. Something had to be done about Pep! So, the governor sent the pup to prison. But this prison pup wasn't really doing time. Instead, he arrived as one of the country's first therapy dogs—dogs that help people by providing comfort and friendship. Pep didn't live in a cell; he was allowed to wander the prison and its yard freely, raising the spirits of prisoners and guards. Everyone loved this "bad dog"; he cheered up lonely prisoners and acted as a companion during their long stays. Pep was even reformed himself: He never chewed on another sofa cushion again! Even better, he inspired an entire future of therapy dogs.

MERCURY

UNDERWATER AGENTS

ZAK TRAINS WITH SPECIAL EQUIPMENT.

K-DOG, ZAK

It started in secret in 1960. The U.S. Navy wanted to improve its sonar abilities so its submarines could dive faster and deeper. It found a good instructor: the bottlenose dolphin. Studying dolphins helped the Navy improve its technology, and also sparked another idea. The Navy started training marine mammals to serve. Dolphins, beluga whales, sea lions, and other marine mammals learned to perform various tasks, from delivering equipment to divers to locating and retrieving lost objects. Some even guarded boats and submarines and performed underwater surveillance with a camera held in their mouths. K-Dog the dolphin learned to find and mark underwater mines and served as a minesweeper in the Arabian Gulf. Zak, a sea lion, has been trained to apprehend hostile divers underwater. These animals take their "serve and protect" motto seriously!

ZAK

Military dolphins are trained a lot like police dogs are—they receive a reward (like fish!) when they complete a task.

K-DOG

READY FOR DUTY!

WHOSE SHADOW IS *THAT?*

PUNXSUTAWNEY PHIL

Since 1887, Punxsutawney Phil has "predicted" an early spring only 17 times.

If you're going to speak with Punxsutawney Phil, it helps if you speak "Groundhogese." That's the language of the groundhog—or so the story goes. And the most important time to have a conversation with Phil is on February 2, or Groundhog Day, when, according to the legend, Phil makes a very important prediction. On that day, in Punxsutawney, Pennsylvania, U.S.A., you'll find Phil living in a place called Gobbler's Knob. He's usually surrounded by important townsfolk. What does a groundhog talk about? Well, early in the morning, Phil crawls out of his burrow and tells the townsfolk whether or not he's seen his shadow. If he's seen it, there will be an early spring. If not, it's six more weeks of winter! Now, to hear the townsfolk tell it, there is and only ever has been *one* Phil. True, the life span of an average groundhog is only six years or so. But Punxsutawney Phil has been making his annual prediction for more than 130 years!

TARO AND JIRO: SURVIVORS

Taro and Jiro were brothers and during one harsh winter, they became survivors. These legendary huskies were part of a Japanese expedition to Antarctica in 1957 supporting researchers based at Syowa Station, a research facility on a small island where temperatures can dip below minus 10°F (-23°C). An unusually harsh winter that year forced an evacuation. There was no room on the helicopter for the dogs, so Taro and Jiro were left behind with some food. The plan was to return a few days later to get them, but an unexpected storm changed those plans. An expedition did not reach the base for another 11 months. No one dared hope that the dogs had survived. But when the new team finally arrived, who was there to greet them? Taro and Jiro! Those clever dogs had taught themselves to hunt penguins and seals. They had survived impossible odds by relying on each other. And they taught the world a lasting lesson about canine loyalty and the power of friendship. In fact, Taro and Jiro were so remarkable that they became unofficial national symbols of Japan and inspired several monuments and two movies. Their bond has stood the test of time to this very day!

JIRO

TARO

TITANOBOA

THE KING OF
SNAKES

Giant, 40-foot (12-m)-long snakes: Do they exist? Not anymore, but 60 million years ago the enormous *Titanoboa*—which was longer than a school bus and weighed more than a ton (0.9 t)—slithered across prehistoric Earth, stalking shallow waters and dining on crocodiles for breakfast! Discovered in Colombia, South America, in 2009, the serpent was twice as long as any snake living today and four times as heavy as the giant anaconda. In fact, it was larger than most scientists thought possible for a snake. So just how did this ancient snake species get to be so big? Scientists asked themselves the same question. For an oversize, cold-blooded reptile like *Titanoboa* to thrive, prehistoric Colombia had to be hot and humid. But a lot more hot and humid than scientists thought it had been. Were experts wrong about the past? Much of what scientists thought they knew about prehistoric temperatures and habitats has been called into question. Finding *Titanoboa* didn't solve any mysteries. Instead, it opens up more questions, changes what scientists know about snakes past and present, and ultimately, may change what we know about the prehistoric world.

BIG THANKS TO YOU, MY LAD!

JACK WAS A TURKEY LIKE THE ONE PICTURED HERE.

"Pardoned" White House turkeys live out the remainder of their lives at Mount Vernon, George Washington's historic estate in Virginia.

A PARDON
FOR JACK

Turkeys everywhere may feel a special kinship with U.S. president Abraham Lincoln's son Tad. In 1863, Lincoln signed an official proclamation setting aside the last Thursday in November as a "day of Thanksgiving and Praise." Not long after, a citizen sent a live turkey to the White House to be part of a Christmas holiday feast. Ten-year-old Tad was delighted. He named the turkey Jack and taught Jack to follow him around the White House grounds. Then Tad learned that Jack was on the menu for the feast. Lincoln was in the middle of an important meeting when Tad burst in. He begged his father to spare the turkey. Unable to say no to his beloved son, Lincoln wrote "an order of reprieve" for Jack. Tad dashed to the kitchen in time to stop Jack from being added to the menu. Success! Tad had saved his friend. He had also secured the White House's very first pardon for a turkey. More than 100 years later, President George H. W. Bush officially began the American tradition of the presidential pardoning of a turkey at Thanksgiving, which continues to this day.

BOBBIE
THE WONDER DOG

It was supposed to be a fun road trip: Frank and Elizabeth Brazier set out from their home in Silverton, Oregon, U.S.A., during summer 1923. They were on the way to their old hometown, Wolcott, Indiana, with their dog, Bobbie. They were almost to Wolcott when it happened: Bobbie got separated from the family at a gas station. They searched and searched as long as they could, but there was no sign of him anywhere. With heavy hearts, they continued on. Six months later, one of Elizabeth's daughters was walking through Silverton when she spotted something in the middle of the street. It looked half-starved. Its feet were raw. Its fur was matted and full of burrs. Despite its rough appearance, she would have known this creature anywhere: Bobbie! From the moment he became lost, Bobbie had been trying to get back to his family. He never gave up. He walked through blazing deserts and snowy mountains—always homeward. Word of his loyalty, determination, and faithfulness spread. Bobbie changed the world's thinking on what it means to truly be man's best friend.

BOBBIE

Bobbie logged more than 2,500 miles (4,023 km). He averaged 14 miles (22.5 km) a day.

THE
OLD BLACKS

THE OLD BLACKS

They served during World War I at the front lines. They also served at the rear. They served together, always. And perhaps most miraculous of all, they came home together, too. They were "the Old Blacks," a nickname given to a team of six gun horses. These amazing equines began their service in 1914 in France and Belgium. By November 1917, the number of horses and mules in use by the British Army alone was a million or more. Teams were yoked together to pull heavy guns, to haul ammunition wagons, to transport food and supplies, and to collect the wounded and dead from the battlefields. Horses often toiled in the open, completing tasks in the face of relentless enemy fire. It was dangerous work, but the human soldiers depended on it—and perhaps none were more dependable than the Old Blacks. Four of the brave horses were wounded in battle—one horse was wounded three times. Yet the team stayed together and pressed on, saving countless lives. And when the war ended in 1918, all six horses returned home to England, together still.

ANIMAL HEROES

Heroes come in all shapes and sizes, from furry to feathered! These three selfless animals arrived in the nick of time, proving themselves to truly be humankind's best friends.

BALTO

MISSION OF MERCY

TOGO

Nome, Alaska's Dr. Curtis Welch knew what he faced. Two young patients had diphtheria, a deadly and highly contagious disease. Without medicine, the town's entire population of 1,400 was at risk. The nearest batch of lifesaving serum waited in Anchorage. More than 20 mushers and their sled dog teams would take part in a sort of relay called the "Great Race of Mercy" to deliver the serum. They were off, and racing against time. The country's most famous musher, Leonhard Seppala, decided to take a risky shortcut over a frozen body of water, called Norton Sound, in a gale. Seppala's lead dog was 12-year-old Siberian husky Togo. Togo and his 19 fellow dogs struggled for traction. The fierce winds threatened to break apart the ice and send the team adrift at sea. Racing madly under brutal conditions, they made it to the coastline only hours before the ice cracked! The precious package was handed off for the last time to a musher named Gunnar Kaasen. Kaasen's team, led by 6-year-old Balto, set off into a blinding blizzard. Before long, Kaasen could no longer navigate. He almost gave up hope, but Balto knew the trail well. In near-total whiteout conditions for 20 hours, Balto led his team the final 53 miles (85 km). On February 2, 1925, at 5:30 a.m., the nearly frozen dogs arrived in Nome. The dogs were too tired to even bark, but the serum had successfully been delivered, and they had saved the town.

The total distance the mushers traveled was 674 miles (1,085 km).

LULU TO THE RESCUE!

Luke Richards was just a teenager when he found a baby kangaroo, called a joey, on a road in Australia. The joey's mom had been hit by a car. Luke knew the joey would die without her mom, so he took her home and named her Lulu. Luke's parents, Len and Lynn, were surprised to find a baby kangaroo in their son's room! But they were proud of Luke for rescuing her. At that time, no one could have known that Lulu would one day return the favor. Years later, Len was inspecting a damaged tree with Lulu by his side. Suddenly, a large branch came loose from the tree and struck Len on the head! He fell to the ground. Kangaroos don't normally make many sounds, but Lulu started croaking and barking as loudly as she could to call the family. She also used her big feet to hold Len safely on his side. His family came running, and Len was rushed to the hospital, where he made a full recovery. Lulu's loyalty and quick thinking saved Len's life. In return, Lulu was given an award called the Animal Valor Award to honor her bravery—the first time it was given to a wild animal.

LULU

MONTY SAVES THE DAY

It was the middle of the night, and Patricia Peter was fast asleep. But her ginger tabby cat, Monty, began nibbling on the fingers of her left hand—the same hand that Patricia uses to test her blood sugar levels to monitor her diabetes. Patricia tried to go back to sleep, but Monty refused to be ignored until Patricia sat up. Suddenly, she felt very dizzy. Her legs felt weak and she felt nauseated. What was wrong? Monty began meowing and rubbing against her leg, directing Patricia toward the kitchen. She blindly followed. Monty sprinted ahead and sat down next to the diabetic testing kit Patricia used to test her blood sugar levels. She knew what he was telling her to do. A normal blood sugar range was between 5 and 7, but the test showed that her levels had fallen to 2.7! Monty waited by her side while she took some medicine, and after 15 minutes, her blood sugar level came back to a healthy range. She was safe! Without Monty to warn her, Patricia might have fallen into a diabetic coma or had a diabetic seizure. Monty had saved her life.

When Monty worries about Patricia, he will put his face close to her mouth to smell her breath. He can detect changes in her blood sugar levels before she can feel them!

MONTY

Three-fingered sloths have nine vertebrae, allowing them to rotate their heads up to 300 degrees.

BUTTERCUP:
SUPER SLOTH

Judy Avey-Arroyo didn't know who—or what—to expect when three girls knocked on her door in 1992. They were cradling something wrapped in a blanket. Was it a baby? Sort of: It was an orphaned baby sloth, and the girls asked Avey-Arroyo to take care of it. At the time, Avey-Arroyo and her husband ran a small hotel in Costa Rica. She didn't know anything about sloths. But she helped the girls anyway and took the poor baby sloth. Then she began calling veterinarians for advice: What do sloths eat? How much sleep do they need? But no one seemed to know. So, Judy and the sloth, which she named Buttercup, learned together. Buttercup bloomed into a healthy youngster, and before long, another orphan sloth appeared on her doorstep. And another, and another! No challenge proved too tough for Judy. She eventually opened Sloth Sanctuary to care for injured and orphaned sloths. With Buttercup guiding her, Avey-Arroyo discovered much of what we know about sloths today.

BUTTERCUP

WINKIE: SEA RESCUE

WINKIE

In 1942 a badly damaged British WWII bomber ditched into the North Sea, and the crew of four plummeted into freezing waters more than 100 miles (161 km) from home. Unable to radio their position back to base, they were in grave danger. The men had only one hope: the pigeon that was on board their plane had been thrown loose from her container. Her wings were coated with oil from the wreckage, but the little bird took flight anyway. She carried no message, but when she was finally intercepted, the British were able to calculate the position of the downed aircraft by using the time difference between the plane's crash and the arrival of the bird. They even factored in wind direction and the amount of oil on the bird's feathers! A rescue mission was launched, and the men were found within 15 minutes. The pigeon had saved the lives of the nearly frozen crew.

Winkie's real "name" was NEHU 40 NS1. She received her nickname after an injury during her heroic flight led her to wink often.

DOGS IN SPACE

Belka and Strelka were taking a road trip … without the road. On August 19, 1960, after some hard training, these two Soviet stray dogs launched into space on Sputnik 5 and would become the first living creatures to orbit and safely return to Earth! Think of the excitement of the trip! Think of the fame and fortune that would follow! As it turned out, Belka was not a fan of space travel; she'd rather keep her paws on Mother Earth. During their daylong flight, she barked a lot and even got a bit motion sick. Strelka didn't seem to mind her travels, though. After orbiting for nearly 25 hours and circling Earth 18 times, the dogs landed safely back home. Belka and Strelka paved the way: Eight months after their successful mission, cosmonaut Yuri Gagarin became the first human to orbit Earth and return safely.

Belka and Strelka did not go into space alone. With them on Sputnik 5 were 42 mice and a couple of rats. All were unharmed by their one-day voyage.

BELKA   STRELKA

PAUL

PSYCHIC PAUL

Paul was a gambler. He especially liked placing the big bets on World Cup soccer matches. He was good at it, too. When he picked a side, people took notice and followed his lead. Which was unusual considering Paul was an *octopus* at the Sea Life Centre in Oberhausen, Germany! Paul's keepers had him predict the outcomes of the German national football team's international matches. To do this, they gave Paul two boxes containing food. The boxes were identical except that each had one flag for the teams competing in an upcoming match. Whichever box Paul ate from counted as his prediction for the winner. Sounds silly, right? Except that Paul chose correctly more than 85 percent of the time. This amazing octopus correctly predicted the winning team in four of Germany's six 2008 Euro matches, and all seven of their matches in the 2010 World Cup! No one could explain it, but people everywhere cheered for the winners—and for Paul!

A dog's nose is more sensitive than a human's, and has up to 300 million olfactory receptors. People have about 6 million.

KAI

KAI: FIRE DOG

An animal shelter was no place for a dog like Kai. The staff could tell that this dog was smart; she had something special. So they called the State Farm Arson Dog Program, and Kai began her career as a fire dog. There she learned to sniff out things that can start fires, like gasoline. But her real skill is staying calm and focused amid the heat, smoke, spraying water, bright lights, and sirens on the scene of a real fire. With a single command—"Seek!"—Kai goes to work. If she smells something suspicious, Kai signals her human partner by sitting down and pointing to a spot with her nose. So far, she has worked more than 200 fire-and bomb-related investigations across Texas. Her super-sniffing detective work might make someone think twice before starting a fire in her state!

COPYCAT IS JUST LIKE "REGULAR" CATS, LIKE THE ONE HERE.

COPY CAT

In 2001, scientists in Texas announced that they had cloned the first pet—a cat they named Copy Cat. This was big news! Previous mammal clones had been barnyard animals, like cows and goats. House pets had never been successfully cloned. Although Copy Cat's existence is wildly exciting to the scientific world, her life so far has been rather quiet. She was adopted, settled in with her cat partner, Smokey, and had a litter of three kittens: Tess, Tim, and Zip. Considering their mother's origins, all three kittens were remarkably unremarkable. Still, the science behind Copy Cat's birth has big implications for conservation. In India, where the cheetah population has been entirely wiped out, the country announced plans to use this same technology to clone cheetahs! They aim to use genetic material from Asiatic cheetahs in Iran to clone new Indian cheetahs. From house cats to wild cheetahs ... imagine which species might be saved next by the Copy Cat cloning technology!

A clone is never actually identical because different environments affect an animal's personality.

2000 mL
KIMAX®
KIMBLE USA

TAMWORTH TWO:
THE GREAT ESCAPE

It could have been the plot of a cops and robbers movie: a brother-and-sister team on the run with the police in hot pursuit. Only this brother and sister just happened to be Tamworth pigs! Named after the infamous outlaws Butch Cassidy and the Sundance Kid, the porcine siblings were five months old when they fled the truck taking them to a slaughterhouse in the U.K. Their clever attempts to elude capture—it took six days to get them—were carefully recorded by the media. The pigs' getaway involved squeezing through a fence and swimming across a river. From there, the trail went cold. They seemed to have disappeared, but in truth, the escapees were receiving help! The pigs had been hiding in the garden of local residents who refused to report the pigs until a national newspaper guaranteed their safety. It worked: The pigs got a new home at an animal sanctuary and had long lives. The memorable duo definitely left their mark while they were on the run!

RIP THE RESCUE DOG

As a stray mutt during World War II in London, Rip probably wanted an owner and affection. But this determined dog also seemed to want something more—a job! When Air Raid warden E. King discovered Rip after a heavy London bombing in 1940, he fed the dog a few scraps and expected him to move along. Rip had something else in mind, though, and set to work as an unofficial rescue dog. Between 1940 and 1941, Rip found more than a hundred trapped victims, setting a new standard. Before he came along, human rescuers merely listened for cries or tapping from survivors to locate them. Rip's sensitive nose proved stronger than human ears, allowing rescuers to find survivors without relying on noise. But he was more than just his nose: Rip was courageous, working in dangerous post-bombing conditions amid fire, smoke, and heat. He hunted for survivors in crumbling bricks and charred, unstable ruins. His fearlessness inspired other rescuers to work harder, search longer, and save more people. In the end, Rip had found himself more than a job; he found true purpose!

CLEVER HANS THE COUNTING HORSE

What's two times two? That's easy: four. If the eighth day of the month is a Tuesday, what is Friday's date? The 11th. Those questions probably don't seem too hard to answer. But could you answer them if you were a *horse?* Clever Hans could! In 1904, Germany was abuzz over mathematics teacher Wilhelm von Osten's horse. Word had it that Hans could add, subtract, multiply, divide, tell time, keep track of a calendar, read, and even spell just by tapping his hoof. Surely this was a trick created by von Osten, right? Well, a famous scientist was determined to get to the bottom of it. So he set up a test for Hans. Fans were shocked when Hans didn't pass! It turned out that this smart steed needed two things to succeed: He had to be able to *see* the questioner, and the questioner had to *know* the correct answer. Hans was actually reading the body language and facial expressions of his examiner. The person testing Hans was tipping off the horse without knowing it! Hans might not have known the real answers, but he was clever indeed, and taught the world much about animal intelligence.

Rip received a medal of honor for his bravery in 1945.

RIP

CONGO

THE EYE OF THE BEHOLDER

Congo's sense of composition would have been impressive for any artist, but it was especially remarkable because he was a chimpanzee! When zoologist and anthropologist Desmond Morris first offered Congo a pencil and paper in the late 1950s, no one expected much. But Congo began creating. By the age of four, he had made 400 drawings and paintings. Eventually, Congo's work gained fame, and even appeared in an exhibit at the Institute of Contemporary Arts in London. Many people loved his paintings, but not all—some questioned whether the pieces were truly even art. But whether or not it was "art," Congo had created a sensation. His paintings drew more conversation than many humans' art, and sparked the important question: What is art? The debate continues to this day.

Spanish painter Pablo Picasso was reportedly a fan of Congo's work. He hung one of the ape's pictures on his studio wall after receiving it as a gift.

GRIZZLY
GUEST

When naturalist Casey Anderson "adopted" a bear named Brutus, he might not have realized what he was getting into. He knew plenty about grizzly bears—he just didn't realize how much of a part of his family Brutus would become. Brutus was orphaned in Bozeman, Montana, U.S.A., when he was five months old. Without his mother's guidance, the little cub could never survive in the wild. So, Anderson took him in—literally. Brutus slept in their house, ate at their table, and even swam in their pool! Eventually, at around 800 pounds (362 kg), Brutus got too big to live safely in their house. That's when Anderson founded the Montana Grizzly Encounter rescue and education sanctuary—a place where orphaned bears like Brutus can live safely in a natural habitat. Brutus has more room to roam now, as do the seven other bears that live there. And Anderson and other naturalists can continue learning about grizzlies, all thanks to one unusual pet adoption!

BRUTUS

WILLIE: PARAMEDIC PARROT

Willie, a bright green Quaker parrot, is a pretty smart bird. He knows a lot of words and phrases, from "Mama" to "I love you." But until one terrible day in November 2008, no one was aware that Willie also knew the word "baby." Megan Howard lived in Colorado and was babysitting her roommate's two-year-old daughter, Hannah. Hannah was watching TV and eating a snack when Megan left the room a moment. And that's when Willie started screaming, "Mama, baby! Mama, baby!" over and over while flapping his wings. Megan came running and found Hannah choking on her snack. Megan quickly performed the Heimlich maneuver to dislodge the food blocking Hannah's airway. Willie had often called Megan "Mama," but no one had ever heard him say the word "baby" before. His quick thinking saved Hannah from choking!

WILLIE

WILLIE WAS GIVEN THE RED CROSS ANIMAL LIFESAVER AWARD AT A "BREAKFAST OF CHAMPIONS" EVENT.

YORKIE DOODLE DANDY

Smoky the Yorkie was so tiny she easily fit inside American soldier Corporal William A. Wynne's helmet. He bought her from a buddy who found her in an abandoned foxhole during World War II in the jungles of New Guinea. She weighed only four pounds (1.8 kg), and how she'd ended up there or to whom she belonged remained a mystery. She didn't seem to understand commands in English or in Japanese. For the next two years, Smoky backpacked through the jungle with Wynne and his unit. She slept in Wynne's tent and shared his rations. More than a petite companion, she turned out to be a big help to her fellow soldiers. Once, the men needed to string an important communications wire through a narrow pipe under an airstrip and only Smoky was small enough to fit into the pipe. At Wynne's command, she squeezed in and carried the cable tied to her collar for 70 feet (21.3 m). Problem solved!

Smoky survived 150 air raids on New Guinea and even made it through a typhoon at Okinawa, Japan.

SMOKY

G.I. JOE

A number of animals in this book were awarded the Dickin Medal, the highest award an animal can receive for bravery.

PIGEON PATROL

Homing pigeons are one of the oldest means of long-distance communication, and historically were used in wars. Delivering messages under wartime conditions put pigeon lives at risk. They faced bad weather, night flying, and attacks from birds of prey, in addition to the dangers of military fighting. Thousands of soldiers, airmen, and sailors owe their lives to these small animals.

G.I. JOE

During a key battle over the Italian city Calvi Vecchia in World War II, communications had broken down between British and American Allied troops. While battling for control of Italy, the British had succeeded in breaking through the enemy German line. There was only one small problem: The U.S. Air Force planned to bomb Calvi Vecchia to drive back the enemy. They had no way of knowing the British had already successfully taken the city. British and Italian lives were on the line. The only chance of stopping the American bombers? A borrowed American pigeon named G.I. Joe. British troops hoped the bird could reach the U.S. base before it was too late. With time ticking, G.I. Joe flew a mile a minute for 20 miles (32 km). It was a close call: Bombers were moving down the runway when G.I. Joe arrived, and the message was removed from his leg without a moment to spare. The Air Force quickly called off the attack, sparing the lives of as many as 1,000 British troops and Italian civilians. Go, Joe!

G.I. Joe was the only American animal to receive the Dickin Medal.

COMMANDO: PIGEON IMPOSSIBLE!

During World War II, British prime minister Winston Churchill created the Special Operations Executive (SOE). These men and women were sent behind enemy lines in Europe to complete missions deemed "impossible" by others. When on a mission, they often traveled with the most trustworthy pigeons, who carried vital information back to Britain. The SOE pigeons faced some of the most dangerous assignments, and only one in eight survived missions that started behind enemy lines. A pigeon named Commando may have been the SOE's toughest bird, completing more than 90 crucial missions. His messages identified the positions of German troops, delivered the locations of injured British soldiers and where to rescue them, and even detailed German sites that were used as weapon factories. Without a doubt, Commando's stealth and skill saved many lives and contributed to Britain's war effort.

Commando received the Dickin Medal in 1942.

CHER AMI

A team of Army medics nursed Cher Ami back to health and even fitted him with a carved wooden leg.

CHER AMI

The U.S. 77th Division was surrounded in the Argonne Forest during World War I in northeastern France. Their situation was dire: They were trapped on all sides, their food supplies dwindling, and the nearest source of clean water stood in range of enemy fire. And worse, they were falling under accidental fire from allies. The soldiers had little reason for hope. Seven pigeons had been sent, but all were feared captured, killed, or lost. One last messenger, Cher Ami, had an urgent message strapped to his leg: "We are along road parallel 276.4. Our own artillery is dropping a barrage directly on us. For heaven's sake, stop it." Cher Ami flew away from the safety of the hill into a barrage of gunfire. Twenty-five minutes and 25 miles (40 km) later, he arrived at headquarters. He'd been shot, partially blinded, and received severe wounds to the leg holding the message. But he completed his mission, and the artillery redirected its fire to enemy targets. Reinforcements rushed in. A single pigeon rescued nearly 200 soldiers.

PIGEON MESSAGE

RECEIVED AT MESSAGE CENTER 4:22 PM

TO C. O. 308th INFANTRY

FROM 1st BN 308th INFANTRY

WE ARE ALONG THE ROAD PARALELL 276.4. OUR AR ILLERY IS DROPPING A BARRAGE DIRECTLY ON US. FOR HEAVENS SAKE STOP IT.

WHITTLESAY
MAY 308th

BIRD RELEASED 3 P.M.

RECEIVED AT LOFT 4:05 PM.
DISTRIBUTION
G 3/
G 3 BULLETIN BOARD
C OF S
G 2
12 FIELD ARTILLERY BRIGADE
FILE

ANITA

ARABELLA

THE SPIDERS THAT SPUN IN SPACE

Judith Miles, a 17-year-old high school student from Lexington, Massachusetts, U.S.A., was curious. After reading an article in *National Geographic* magazine about how spiders build their webs, she learned that a spider's weight helps it determine how thick a web to weave. Spiders also rely on both wind and gravity to trigger the web-building process. So Judith wondered: Could spiders spin webs while in space, where it's weightless and neither gravity nor wind exist? She proposed that the National Aeronautics and Space Administration (NASA) find out, and they decided to approve the mission. In 1973, Anita and Arabella, both orb weaver spiders, were "recruited" to blast off to the space station, Skylab. Each was given a juicy fly to snack on during the flight. Once aboard Skylab 3, the spiders were closely watched. Could they spin a web that was out of this world? They could, and they did! After a bit of trial and error, Arabella spun the first web. Anita followed with a web of her own. Both webs were thinner than the ones made on Earth, but otherwise, very similar. This was just one of the very first insights into living in space: One small step for spiders, one giant leap for mankind!

Orb weaver spiders eat their old webs to produce fresh silk for new webs.

JUDITH MILES DISCUSSES HER SKYLAB EXPERIMENT WITH MARSHALL SPACE FLIGHT CENTER SCIENTISTS.

TALE OF A WHALE

Humphrey became one of the most famous humpback whales in history—all because he had a terrible sense of direction! He got "lost" *twice*, landing in San Francisco Bay both times. Humphrey first entered the bay in 1985, swimming up the Sacramento River and into Rio Vista, California. Although residents loved seeing a whale up close, they knew Humphrey wasn't supposed to be there. Rescuers led him back to sea by forming a "sound net," which was simply a group of boats full of volunteers that banged on steel pipes to drive him in the opposite direction. Five years later, Humphrey returned and got stuck on a mudflat. This time, the Coast Guard stepped in to help him. Humphrey had many adoring fans, but at least one exhausted rescue worker hoped she'd seen the last of him. Says Peigin Barrett, director of the California Marine Mammal Center: "I don't want to ever see him in San Francisco Bay ever again." Despite any hassles Humphrey may have caused, his frequent visits helped the world learn about humpbacks and feel connected to these magnificent creatures.

HUMPHREY

PETIE THE THERAPY PONY

When it's time to go to work, Petie walks through revolving doors and gets on the elevator like it's no big deal. And it wouldn't be, except that Petie is a pony. But he's not your average pony. As a specially trained therapy pony, Petie visits children in Akron Children's Hospital, and Cleveland's Rainbow Babies & Children's Hospital, where he's been volunteering for almost 20 years. What can a pony do to help sick kids? Plenty! Calm and patient Petie helps others feel that way, too. And he provides physical therapy for children recovering from illness or injury: When they brush Petie or work with his halters, it helps build their strength. Petie also provides companionship and lifts patients' spirits by distracting them from their troubles. He changes their world for the better.

PETIE

Petie is much bigger than a therapy dog, but smaller than a horse. He stands about three feet (1 m) tall and weighs 380 pounds (172 kg).

CAT BURGLAR
(FUR REAL!)

He didn't look much like a thief—he didn't dress in black or wear a mask. In fact, he wore a furry orange coat. But in his neighborhood in Portland, Oregon, Snorri was a known cat burglar. With an emphasis on the *cat!* This feisty feline had developed a deep love for shoes. Sneakers? He adored them. Slippers? You bet. Sandals? Absolutely! He especially loved flip-flops. To build his collection, Snorri started swiping his neighbors' shoes from their yards and carrying them home in his mouth. Soon Snorri's bad habits grew and he started taking more than shoes; he'd carry just about anything home. Snorri's people noticed his stash of shoes, bath towels, dog toys, and gardening gloves growing. Now they post Snorri's "borrowed" items on social media so their neighbors can be reunited with their things. What started out as a crafty cat collection became a way for neighbors to connect and share their lives with each other.

SNORRI

Squatting by a termite mound, David Greybeard picked a blade of grass and poked it into the mound. When he pulled it out, it was covered with delicious termites, which he ate. David Greybeard, a chimpanzee, was not the first chimp to make tools. But he was the first to do it in front of a human. Primatologist Jane Goodall was in Tanzania in 1960 studying chimps. At the time, toolmaking was regarded as a uniquely human ability—one that set humans apart from animals. Through her patient observations, Goodall made many amazing discoveries. But witnessing David Greybeard's toolmaking had an enormous impact in the scientific community. It required scientists to rethink all they thought they knew about animals. When Goodall sent a message to her sponsor, paleoanthropologist Louis Leakey, he telegrammed back:

DAVID GREYBEARD

Goodall also observed chimpanzees eating meat, dispelling the notion that chimps are vegetarians.

NOW WE MUST REDEFINE TOOL

REDEFINE MAN

OR ACCEPT CHIMPANZEES AS HUMAN

DAVID GREYBEARD

ROSELLE
TO THE RESCUE

On September 11, 2001, 19 terrorists hijacked four airplanes and carried out attacks against targets in the United States. Two of the planes flew into the twin towers of the World Trade Center in New York City. The enormous buildings held thousands of people, many of whom were trapped in the burning towers. Roselle had been asleep under her owner's desk on the 78th floor in Tower 1 when the plane struck 15 floors above them. Michael Hingson couldn't see what was going on; he is blind. Chaos, smoke, heat, and confusion surrounded them. Roselle had only one focus: saving Hingson. She calmly guided him to stairwell B and began leading him, along with 30 others, down 1,463 steps. It took them an hour to make the descent. Just as Roselle led Hingson out of the building, Tower 2 collapsed. Continuing her heroic efforts, surrounded by debris and danger, Roselle again guided Hingson to safety.

Roselle later received the Dickin Medal for her bravery.

ROSELLE

WINTER'S TAIL

WINTER

Winter was just a baby when it happened: The little dolphin became tangled up in a crab trap line near Cape Canaveral, Florida, U.S.A. Lucky for her, she was rescued and taken to Clearwater Marine Aquarium. Her injuries were serious. Winter lost the end of her tail, a part called the fluke. To swim naturally, a dolphin moves its tail muscle up and down, and the fluke pushes the dolphin forward. Winter tried swimming without her fluke, but she couldn't swim fast and she couldn't jump high out of the water, either. Then Kevin Carroll, an expert in making artificial limbs, had an idea. His clients were usually human, but he thought he could make something special—a tail for Winter! He spent 18 months creating an amazing appendage just for her. Winter's new tail sticks to her body using suction, and a special sleeve holds it in place without irritating her sensitive skin. Winter can now swim well, and she can even leap into the air! And best of all, what Kevin learned in helping Winter will continue to benefit humans and other animals missing limbs. What a tale!

Bottlenose dolphins like Winter can reach speeds of more than 18 miles an hour (29 km/h) and dive as deep as 853 feet (260 m) below the surface!

WATER BEAR DON'T CARE

In one study, tardigrades were brought back to life after 30 years.

You can boil them, bake them, deep-freeze them, crush them, dehydrate them, or even blast them into space. It doesn't matter. Tardigrades will survive whatever you throw at them! These eight-legged aquatic animals may be small—about .06 inch (1.5 mm) long—but they're nearly indestructible. If you look close—with a microscope—you'll see what ferocious beasts they are. They have claws like bears, daggerlike teeth, and they tear into and suck the juices out of moss and algae! Okay, maybe *that* doesn't sound so fierce. But still— they are the tough cookies of the microscopic world because they can survive anything ... and nobody really knows how or why. All scientists know so far is that when tardigrades get stressed—either from drying out, lack of food, or another stressful situation—they curl up into balls and enter a deep sleep. They can stay in this state for decades, only coming back to life if they make contact with water. Tardigrades are helping us rethink what we know about what it takes to survive and what it might take to survive on another planet.

Tardigrades also go by the names "water bear" and "moss piglet."

SERGEANT RECKLESS

Sergeant Reckless wasn't just a horse; she was also a marine. Nicknamed for her platoon, "Recoilless rifles," she'd been trained to deliver supplies and ammunition to soldiers in the field during the Korean War. Reckless proved to be exceptionally smart—when learning a new route, she only needed to be shown a few times before she could make deliveries on her own. On the night of March 26, 1953, Reckless's skills were put to the test when her unit joined a fierce fight for a group of hills called the Nevada Complex. In the heat of battle, Reckless made 51 solo trips to different gun positions to rearm her men. The noise of heavy gunfire unnerved her, but Reckless's soldiers needed her. She traveled more than 35 miles (56 km) that night. Shrapnel struck her twice, once above the eye and, later, in her side, but she continued on through the 72-hour battle. This horse's reckless courage saved the lives of her men.

Reckless received the Dickin Medal in 2016.

SERGEANT RECKLESS

ELEPHANT
MATRIARCH

The saying goes that "an elephant never forgets." But when it comes to Echo the elephant, *we'll* never forget what she taught the world. Echo was the leader of an elephant family in Kenya's Amboseli National Park. For more than 30 years, expert Cynthia Moss documented Echo's life. Much of what we know today about African elephants came from Echo. She saved her herd from lions, drought, and deadly human neighbors. But above all, Echo was a compassionate and protective mother. When her calf, Ely, was born with crooked front legs, she did not abandon him. Instead, she stayed next to him until his legs grew strong enough to stand. When a rival herd kidnapped her daughter, Ebony, Echo gathered her largest elephants and charged the kidnappers, rescuing Ebony. Echo demonstrated time and again the intense emotional bonds elephants form with each other. She proved to be a great leader and mother—and, for humans, a great teacher.

ECHO

ELY

Echo's clan was made up of about 15 elephants.

CROSSWALK KITTY

Before and after school each day, the loyal safety patrol volunteer stood at his post. Students at Enterprise Middle School in West Richland, Washington State, had come to expect—and even rely on—him. Never mind the fact that this volunteer happened to be a cat named Sable. No one knows why the older black cat decided to be a crosswalk guard. But he was good at it—almost *purr*-fect at keeping a keen eye out for all the students. It didn't take long for the school to make him an honorary member of the patrol. He never missed a day—if the kids had to be out in the snow, the cold, or the rain, then so did he. Sable retired in 2013, after several years on the job. His dedication to his *paws*-ition taught his community a lot about the importance of service and looking out for one another.

SABLE

WASHOE: A CHIMP OF MANY WORDS

To say her own name, Washoe the chimpanzee formed a W with her fingers and flicked her ear. It's something she learned from researchers, Drs. Allen and Beatrix Gardner, in the late 1960s. The Gardners' research broke frontiers, as the remarkable Washoe became the first nonhuman to communicate using American Sign Language. By age five, she had mastered enough signs to capture the world's attention. But her abilities also set off a long-standing debate over nonhuman primates' ability to learn human language. Was Washoe really communicating with humans or merely parroting signs that she had been taught? How much can humans and other apes truly communicate with each other? Washoe certainly contributed to that conversation, and the debate continues to this day.

Washoe loved shoes! If someone came in wearing a new pair, Washoe would ask the wearer to show them to her.

WASHOE

LING-LING

HSING-HSING

PANDAS
OF PEACE

Pandas are almost irresistibly adorable. So when China gave the United States a pair of giant pandas in honor of President Richard Nixon's historic visit in 1972, it was *panda-monium!* Captured from the wild, the two pandas went to the National Zoo in Washington, D.C., where 20,000 visitors came to see them on their first day. The pandas, named Ling-Ling and Hsing-Hsing, immediately became the zoo's top attraction. And the zoo became a leader in giant panda conservation, sharing information with other institutions about this threatened species. China's gift also had a lasting political impact: "Panda diplomacy" strengthened the bond between the two countries. (In exchange for Ling-Ling and Hsing-Hsing, the United States gave China a pair of musk oxen. Who got the better end of *that* deal?)

THE FINAL FRONTIER

Many courageous animals took part in the space programs of the United States and the Soviet Union. The competition between these two countries to be first in space began in August 1955, when the Soviet Union announced its intention to launch an artificial satellite. From that moment on, both countries wanted to be first. The space race was considered important because it showed the world which country had the best science, technology, and economic systems. Now these countries work together, with other nations, to advance human efforts in space exploration and science. But such was not always the case ...

LAIKA:
CANINE COSMONAUT

On October 4, 1957, the Soviet Union shocked the world by launching the first artificial satellite into space. Sputnik 1 looked like a metal beach ball, and was a significant step forward for the Soviet Union in the space race against the United States. Less than a month later, the Soviets launched Sputnik 2, and this mission carried a passenger. Laika, a stray mixed-breed husky, became the first animal to orbit Earth, paving the way for human spaceflight. Laika's flight was the first of its kind, but she did not survive. Many people were saddened by this news, and wondered if it was fair to put animals at risk in the name of science. Others argued that the lessons learned from Laika's flight were invaluable to human explorers, and the debate continues to this day. In the meantime, Laika became a hero to the world and a symbol of manned spaceflight. Scientists still had a lot to learn about safe space travel. More than three years would pass before cosmonaut Yuri Gagarin's first manned orbital spaceflight. He could not have succeeded without Laika.

LAIKA SITS IN A MOCK-UP OF THE SPACECRAFT CABIN.

LAIKA

Laika means "barker" in Russian.

FIRST IN SPACE

Everyone knows that the first animal in space was the Russian dog Laika, right? Well ... that's not exactly correct. Laika, was the first animal to *orbit* Earth. But the first animal in space beat Laika by 10 years, and wasn't a dog. It was a fruit fly! *Several* fruit flies, actually. They launched on February 20, 1947 aboard the U.S. V-2 rocket, shooting up 68 miles (109 km), and reaching an imaginary line called the Karman line. That's where scientists say Earth's atmosphere meets outer space. And it only took 3 minutes and 10 seconds to get there! The mission was designed to study radiation exposure at high altitudes and how the flies would hold up during the flight. The flies may have been bewildered by their wild ride, but they all lived—proving that living things could survive a trip to space.

ASTRONAUTS CHANGE OUT FOOD TRAYS FOR THE FRUIT FLIES.

SPACE MONKEYS

They made quite a pair: Able was a seven-pound (3-kg) American-born rhesus monkey; Baker was an 11-ounce (310-g) squirrel monkey from Peru. Together, they made up NASA's crew aboard the new Jupiter rocket. Wearing special space suits and placed in a custom-built capsule in the rocket's nose cone, the animals were ready for their May 28, 1959, spaceflight. Scientists would closely monitor the monkeys, watching their vital signs, mental states, and the cabin environment during the more than 15-minute flight. The monkeys traveled at speeds of more than 10,000 miles an hour (16,093 km/h) and reached an altitude of 300 miles (483 km)—that's about 55 times as high as Mount Everest! They successfully withstood forces 38 times the normal pull of gravity on Earth. Able and Baker were weightless for approximately nine minutes. Both monkeys returned safely to Earth, and their mission marked the first successful recovery of living beings after their return from space.

ABLE

ABLE IN A CAPSULE FOR A PRE-FLIGHT TEST.

CANINE DETECTS CANCER

A dog's sense of smell is much better than a human's. A dog can detect a drop of blood in an Olympic-size swimming pool.

When a local animal shelter rescued John D the border collie at six weeks old, people already knew that he was special. So, he was trained to be a search and rescue dog. John D has been called upon to help police with kidnappings, drownings, and missing persons cases, and he's been honored many times for his work. But believe it or not, these feats aren't what John D is *best* known for. This dog has another gift: John D can detect cancer. He picks up the scent from patients' blood or urine samples. Doctors don't really know what John D is smelling when he detects cancer, but they do know his accuracy rate is an amazing 95 percent. John D's inspiring work allows doctors to treat their patients earlier, which can make a big difference in battling the disease. From rescue to rescuer, John D is definitely special!

JOHN D

THE CINDERELLA HORSE

SNOWMAN

Snowman had been a plow horse, and not an especially good one. He was on his way to the slaughterhouse when a riding instructor named Harry de Leyer bought him for $80. At first, de Leyer used Snowman to teach children how to ride, and then he sold Snowman to a neighbor. But the sale didn't stick. Snowman leaped over a high fence and ran the six miles (9.6 km) back home! De Leyer saw something different in his horse after that and began training him to be a show jumper. De Leyer taught Snowman how to *fly*. Within two years, Snowman was winning prestigious contests as a jumper and performing jaw-dropping stunts, like jumping over other horses! Everyone from socialites to taxi drivers loved Snowman universally, inspired by his winning spirit and rags-to-riches leap to stardom.

GUSTAV: D-DAY DELIVERY

The World War II Battle of Normandy—also known as D-Day—began June 6, 1944. More than 150,000 American, British, and Canadian forces landed on five beaches along a stretch of the heavily fortified French coast. The invasion remains one of the largest amphibious military assaults in history. But it was up to a tiny pigeon named Gustav to deliver news of the attack strapped to his leg. The fearless bird flew into a 30-mile-an-hour (48-km/h) headwind and enemy fire. Heavy clouds obscured his path. Yet, nothing would stop Gustav. Somehow he flew the 150 miles (241 km) to his destination in just five hours and 16 minutes—an incredible distance under such brutal conditions. Gustav's message brought the first word of the invasion to the British mainland, delivering news the world desperately needed.

Gustav was awarded a Dickin Medal in 1944 for his tenacity.

GUSTAV

HAVING FAITH

Faith, the vicar's cat at St. Augustine's Church in London, typically slept upstairs. But on the night of September 6, 1940, Faith carried her kitten down three flights of stairs and tucked her baby into a little pigeonhole in a wall the vicar used for storage. Why the unusual behavior? Perhaps she had a sixth sense about danger. The vicar tried four times to put the kitten back in its basket upstairs. And four times, Faith carried it down to the hole again. Three days later, the church was bombed while the vicar was out. Fire raged as Faith hunkered down with her kitten, the church's walls and roof collapsing around them. Miraculously, both she and her kitten remained unharmed and were rescued the next morning! In a time of great danger and uncertainty, Faith's intuition and determination to protect her young struck a deep chord with the entire town. After that, everyone tried to have just a little more faith.

FAITH

SPACE JELLIES

THE SHUTTLE WAS FILLED WITH JELLYFISH LIKE THE ONE PICTURED HERE.

In 1991, NASA had an interesting—and *strange*—idea: It sent 2,478 baby jellyfish into space on a shuttle in containers of artificial seawater. They could swim freely and reproduce. By the end of the mission, some 60,000 jellies were orbiting Earth! NASA was trying to learn a few things. First, could a baby jelly develop normally in space? Second, would the lack of gravity affect a jelly's ability to swim? Well, the jellies had no problem developing into adults. They did, however, swim a little funny after they got back to Earth! Jellyfish use a sensor in their bodies to go up or down. These sensors rely on gravity. Without gravity, the space jellies didn't fully develop their sensors. So, when they came back to Earth, NASA saw some silly swimming from those guys! That was important news. Although humans and jellies don't have much in common, they do both have sensors. Humans have them in their inner ears. NASA now needs to know: Would humans raised in space have difficulties with their balance? By studying these jellyfish, NASA can better prepare for a far-off future of mankind in space.

ENDAL
THE LIFESAVER

After a serious injury, Royal Navy chief petty officer Allen Parton couldn't remember anything—not even his wife or kids. He went through years of therapy, but still had trouble walking, talking, and remembering. Then came Endal, a service dog. Assigned to help Parton live a more functional life, Endal could go shopping, use an ATM card, operate an elevator, and even work a washing machine. But Endal did something far more important: He saved Parton's life. One day, a passing car knocked Parton out of his wheelchair in a parking lot. Endal pulled an unconscious Allen into a recovery position and fetched a blanket to cover his friend. Then he ran for help at a nearby hotel. Endal saved Parton! As word of Endal's heroism spread, Parton and Endal received a lot of attention, and Parton, who'd had such difficulty speaking, now had a story he was happy to tell. His relationship with Endal saved him and his family in more ways than one.

ENDAL

FIONA

Fiona comes from the word for "fair" in Gaelic, a language historically spoken by Irish and Scottish people.

FABULOUS FIONA

Fiona was the first Nile hippo born at the Cincinnati Zoo in 75 years.

When Fiona was born, she weighed only 29 pounds (13 kg). That might seem big for a baby, but not if you're a hippopotamus—the average baby hippo can weigh three times that! Fiona was born six weeks early at the Cincinnati Zoo in Ohio, U.S.A., and was barely able to walk or nurse after birth. The zoo flew into action: A round-the-clock team cared for her. They fed her. They held her. They bathed her. She was so fragile, no one knew if she would survive. But Fiona was a fighter. She slowly began to gain weight and soon took her first wobbly steps. The happy hippo grew stronger each day, and her team was there to root for her. Along the way, Fiona's team expanded. It wasn't just the zookeepers and volunteers. It wasn't just the zoogoers. Soon the whole world was watching Fiona over live footage that broadcast her every move. She had had a tough start in life, but she didn't let that stop her: Fiona mugged for the camera, turned somersaults underwater, cheekily teased her parents, and lived life to the fullest. Her zest for life, fighter's spirit, and adorable face were causing a sensation—Fiona even starred in her own online TV show. Who knew the world would be so touched by a little hippo!

MURDER BY MONKEY

Could a primate really be responsible for changing world history? Greece's King Alexander found out the hard way in 1920. While they were walking in his gardens one fateful day, Alexander's dog picked a fight with another of Alexander's pets: a monkey. When the king tried to break up the fight, a second monkey swooped in and bit him. The wounds became infected, and Alexander passed away soon after. His sudden death meant Alexander's father, Constantine I, was reinstated as king. Unfortunately, Constantine led his country into a war against Turkey, which Greece lost. Without that monkey's interference, the two countries may never have gone to war at all—and history might have been different.

KING ALEXANDER (RIGHT) HAD A PET MONKEY LIKE THE ONE SEEN HERE.

UNSINKABLE SAM

If cats have nine lives, Unsinkable Sam used up at least three during his strange military career during World War II. Sam started off in the Nazi fleet on board the *Bismarck*, but ended up serving the Royal Navy on the H.M.S. *Cossack* and the H.M.S. *Ark Royal*. All three ships sank, yet Sam survived each time! The *Bismarck* was one of Germany's largest battleships, tasked with raiding shipping routes from North America to Great Britain. When the Allies detected and attacked the vessel, it sank, and lucky Sam was picked up by British troops on the destroyer H.M.S. *Cossack*. Sam joined their crew, but not long after, a German U-boat sent a torpedo searing into the *Cossack*. Sam survived *that* explosion, too, and was rescued by the aircraft carrier H.M.S. *Ark Royal*. Barely a month later, the *Ark Royal* was torpedoed. An experienced Sam knew to cling to debris and wait for yet another rescue. At that point, Sam had had enough. The hero was sent back to live the rest of his long lives safely in Britain.

SAM WAS A BLACK-AND-WHITE CAT SIMILAR TO THIS ONE.

THE SILKERS

Spider silk has been used to make fishing nets, blood-clotting bandages, and even high-end handkerchiefs. The British and Americans also used silk to defeat Nazis in World War II. How? By using strands of silk to make crosshairs for the sights in their weapons. Vibrations caused by firing a weapon often caused the existing thin wire target lines to snap, making them less accurate. Spiderwebs are strong but elastic; they stretch tightly but don't often snap. Many types of spiders were used in England, but black widows were commonly used in the American war effort. Each spider could spin up to 180 feet (55 m) of web a week. Given a steady diet of two flies a week, the spiders spun their webs across wire frames. The silk was carefully rewound on cylinders like a spool of thread. The spiders may not have realized their contribution to the war effort, but we haven't forgotten.

THE SPIDERS WERE BLACK WIDOWS LIKE THIS ONE.

Spiders can produce silk as thin as one-fifth the diameter of a human hair, yet it is almost unbreakable. In fact, steel of the same thickness isn't as strong.

BISMARCK

H.M.S. ARK ROYAL

BORN TO LIVE FREE

She had been born wild. But for a short time, Elsa lived with a family of humans. George Adamson was the senior game warden of Kenya's Northern Frontier District, and when a lioness attacked him in 1956, he was forced to shoot her in self-defense. When it was over, Adamson learned the lioness had three cubs. He took the orphans home. Two of the cubs found zoo homes, but Adamson and his wife, Joy, kept one they named Elsa. At first, Elsa lived in the Adamsons' house, like any pet cat. But by the time she was three, she had become a powerful lioness. The Adamsons knew they should no longer keep her. But could she be safely returned to the wild? It had never been done before. George Adamson took Elsa to a remote area of Kenya and patiently encouraged her instinct to hunt and fend for herself, training her to live in the wild again. Eventually, her natural instincts took over, and Elsa became the first captive lion ever successfully freed back into her natural environment. She also became an important symbol to the world, representing every animal's right to live free.

ELSA

The Van Allen radiation belt is a doughnut-shaped belt of charged particles that circles Earth and is held in place by Earth's magnetic field.

UGOLYOK

DOGMONAUTS

Yuri Gagarin became the first human to fly into space on April 12, 1961. He completed a single orbit of Earth in 108 minutes. It was a triumph for human explorers. But was it *safe?* To test how humans might be affected by long-term space flight, the Soviet Union launched two dogs, Veterok and Ugolyok, on a long orbital flight through the Van Allen radiation belt. Not exactly a tourist's vacation spot, but the tiny mutts were doing important work. All space explorers are exposed to certain levels of radiation. Would radiation affect the dogs? To everyone's relief, it did not! The dogs touched down safely 22 days later. Both were a little thirsty, but no worse for the wear. In fact, each later gave birth to litters of healthy puppies! These space travelers held the record for the longest space mission for five years, until Soviet cosmonauts completed a nearly 24-day mission. Still, their flight remains unbeaten for the longest spaceflight by *dogs*.

VETEROK

Veterok means "little wind" and Ugolyok means "little piece of coal."

VETEROK TRIES ON HER SPACE SUIT.

THE GOATS THAT DISCOVERED COFFEE

AND THIS IS HOW WE DISCOVERED COFFEE!

Legend has it that a goat herder named Kaldi was working in Ethiopia during the ninth century. His goats came upon an unfamiliar tree with shiny leaves and red berries—*mmm*. When the goats began nibbling on the berries, Kaldi noticed that his herd suddenly had a lot of energy. The peppy goats pranced about happily; these berries weren't *baaad!* Curious, Kaldi munched on a few berries himself and found that he, too, seemed more alert. Kaldi later told this story to a monk. The monk confessed that he often fell asleep during evening prayers. Maybe these magic berries would help him stay awake? The monk dried some berries, then boiled them to make a delicious drink that we know today as coffee! No one knows if this story is true, but if it is, the world has a herd of goats (and one sleepy monk) to thank!

The average American spends more than $1,000 on coffee each year.

LEGEND SAYS THAT GOATS LIKE THIS ONE FIRST NIBBLED ON COFFEE FRUIT, PICTURED HERE.

FABULOUS FELINES

Whether they changed history by exploring space, acting selflessly, or excelling at hunting, these fuzzy felines are the cat's meow.

PURR-FECT!

SCARLETT

SCARLETT: HEROIC MOTHER

Scarlett lived on the streets in Brooklyn, New York, U.S.A. The pregnant cat took shelter in an empty parking garage during a winter storm to welcome her five kittens into the world. Then Scarlett awoke to an eye-stinging wall of smoke. The garage was on fire! She had one instinct: Save her kittens. Carrying the first in her mouth, Scarlett raced across burning embers. She set her kitten down in safety and turned back into the fire. The brave cat made the journey five times, into and out of the inferno, each time carrying another kitten. Then she collapsed. As firemen were working on extinguishing the blaze, one firefighter heard another sound over the roar of the trucks, sirens, and shouting—a faint cry. He discovered the pile of kittens snuggled in a sooty heap. Nearby lay Scarlett, barely alive. She was badly burned and her paws were crusted with soot, but the firefighters carried Scarlett to her kittens. Though her eyes were blistered shut, she pressed her nose against each, making a silent head count. Satisfied that they were all there, Scarlett purred with exhaustion and relief. Over time, Scarlett's wounds healed. She was adopted by a loving family and lived a long and happy life. Her heroism that night will never be forgotten.

FÉLICETTE: SPACE CAT

Everyone knows that humans have sent animals into space. Dogs, monkeys, rabbits, mice, and more have flown to the stars. But what about ... cats? Of course! By 1963, the French space agency had 14 cats in spaceflight training. These fearless felines endured hours of specialized training to prepare them for the gravity-defying trip to space. Of all the would-be cat-o-nauts, one kitty stood out from all the rest: Félicette. She was a street cat from Paris, but it appeared she had the right *cat*itude for the job. On October 18, 1963, Félicette blasted off aboard a Véronique AG1 rocket. Her flight carried her 130 miles (209 km) above Earth before landing. The trip only took about 15 minutes, but it was a long way to go for a cat. Félicette landed home safe and sound (and presumably on all fours), and her epic journey helped pave the way to our modern understanding of spaceflight and its effects on living things.

SPACE CATS IN FLIGHT CAPSULE

FÉLICETTE ENTERS HER SUIT.

FÉLICETTE

TIBBLES, WREN SLAYER

More than 100 years ago, on Stephens Island off the coast of New Zealand, lived a cat named Tibbles. Tibbles was a lighthouse cat, responsible for keeping the lighthouse free of vermin, and she took her job very seriously. She kept a close eye on the island's wildlife, including a certain small, nocturnal, and flightless bird species. Soon, Tibbles decided that the island wasn't big enough for both cat and bird—and she had no intention of leaving! The lighthouse keeper noticed Tibbles's interest in these feathered friends. Just what was this bird that kept Tibbles so occupied? He decided to send a specimen off to England. The lighthouse keeper was stunned when the bird was declared a new species— dubbed the Stephens Island wren—unknown to science! Unfortunately, this incredible discovery made no impression on Tibbles. She continued to dispatch the birds in droves. And she wasn't alone: Tibbles gave birth to a litter of kittens, and they soon swarmed the area. Legend has it that within a year of Tibbles's arrival, the cats had caught every Stephens Island wren. Just like that, they had wiped out an entire species. *Bad Tibbles!* But despite her overenthusiasm, Tibbles had taught the scientific community a valuable lesson: The introduction of just one species—in this case a curious kitty and some feline friends—into a new place can change the world.

TIBBLES WAS A HOUSECAT LIKE THE ONE PICTURED HERE.

SECRETARIAT

It had been 25 long years since a horse had won the Triple Crown, one of the most coveted achievements in horse racing. Expectations for Secretariat and jockey Ron Turcotte at the Belmont Stakes race couldn't have been higher: Fans counted on them to win. At the sound of the starting gun, Secretariat shot forward. He ran neck and neck with another horse, Sham, for the first quarter of the race. But then, Secretariat began pulling forward. By the time he reached the back stretch of the track, he was so far ahead, he was alone. Secretariat won the race by a jaw-dropping 31 lengths, in what is widely regarded as one of the greatest races of all time. He set a world record, running 1.5 miles (2.4 km) in just 2 minutes 24 seconds. Few in the racing world had ever seen the likes of it; some even say that Secretariat's record will never be broken.

SPACE RAT

HERE HECTOR IS FIT WITH A SPACE SUIT.

HECTOR

Hector was not the first choice for a French space traveler. Other countries were sending dogs and chimpanzees; Hector was a rat. In fact, his lucky day came almost by accident. His training partner liked to chew through the braided wires that recorded his vital signs. The flight was delayed while his wires were repaired, and the wire chewer lost his flying privileges. So, Hector moved into the lead spot aboard France's Véronique rocket on February 22, 1961. The ride was rough but brief. The rocket's engine only fired for 25 seconds before failing. Hector pitched and rolled as he reached an altitude of 93 miles (150 km). Luckily, 8 minutes and 10 seconds after liftoff, a parachute opened, carrying him safely back to Earth. Despite the flight's difficulties, useful data were collected on Hector's brief journey—one more animal contribution to space science—and this time by a rat!

SECRETARIAT

A "length" is a unit of measurement that represents the approximate length of one horse. That distance is easier to judge than yards or feet when horses are flying by at high speed.

NO BETTER DOG

Judy the English pointer was born in Shanghai, but during World War II found herself marooned on an island in the South China Sea with the crew of the Royal Navy ship H.M.S. *Grasshopper.* The entire crew was captured and taken to a notorious prisoner of war camp. During the ordeal, Judy developed a close bond to an airman named Frank Williams. Their special friendship brought them both comfort—and ensured their survival. When a torpedo struck a ship they were on, Williams saved Judy by pushing her through a porthole. Both nearly drowned, but Judy returned the favor by paddling through the water and retrieving pieces of debris for the prisoners to cling to. When Williams and the rest of the crew finally were liberated, he couldn't leave his hero behind. He smuggled Judy aboard a troopship bound for Liverpool! At last, they traveled home together. Judy received the Dickin Medal in 1946.

Judy was the only animal to be registered as an Allied prisoner of war.

JUDY

NO TROUBLE WITH TREO

Treo was Trouble with a capital *T*. As a puppy, this black Labrador mix had a habit of barking and trying to bite anyone who came near him. Treo's owner wasn't sure how to give Treo the discipline he needed—maybe the British Army could help? Yes indeed. There, the enlisted Treo's attitude improved by leaps and bounds. He flew through basic training and was soon ready for advanced work. Under the watchful eye of his new handler, Sergeant Dave Heyhoe, Treo became a "four-legged metal detector." One day while on patrol in Afghanistan, Treo suddenly dropped to the ground and began sniffing the sand. Nobody moved—Heyhoe could tell Treo was detecting something. He had found a string of bombs called a daisy chain; when one bomb is detonated, all the others in the chain explode. There were enough explosives to destroy their camp and harm up to 40 people, but Treo had kept them all safe. A month later, Treo discovered a second daisy chain, saving many more lives. Treo was awarded the Dickin Medal for his attentiveness and devotion to duty. Now Treo is a Hero with a capital *H!*

Labrador retrievers are the most popular breed in the United States.

TREO

SCOTCH LASS

A well-seasoned World War II spy, Scotch Lass made 43 flights from small naval aircraft in the North Sea. In 1944, the plucky pigeon was dropped with an agent into Holland on special duty. Scotch Lass's mission required her to fly intelligence back to England while the agent stayed in place. But the team wouldn't be sending a message back this time; they were after a different kind of intelligence. The agent had obtained photographs of strategic importance, taken by resistance workers. Scotch Lass's flight began terribly: In semidarkness of predawn, Scotch Lass flew directly into telegraph wires. Despite severe injuries, she carried on and completed her mission, flying more than 250 miles (400 km). She delivered 38 photographs—an important development for carrier pigeons and the war effort.

REGAL RHINO

Clara came from humble beginnings, orphaned when hunters shot her mother. These sad things happened to rhinoceroses in India in the 1740s. What had never happened before was a rhinoceros touring Europe—but that's exactly what Clara did next. When Dutchman Douwemout Van der Meer, a ship's captain from the Netherlands, saw people's reactions to his exotic "pet," he decided to take Clara to Europe. There, she quickly became a celebrity. She fascinated public crowds and had audiences with rulers. Clara even started a fashion rage in Paris, with wigs styles "a la rhinoceros." For the next 17 years, Clara traveled all over Europe. What drew the crowds to her? Was it her exotic, armor-plated body? Or her calm and regal demeanor? No one can say. But she remained in demand for the rest of her days and gained much needed attention for rhinoceroses everywhere.

Clara required 70 pounds (32 kg) of hay, 25 pounds (11 kg) of bread, and 14 buckets of water PER DAY.

CLARA WAS A RHINOCEROS LIKE THE ONE SEEN HERE.

Since 1997, these furry super sniffers have helped clear more than 13,200 mines from minefields in Tanzania, Mozambique, Angola, and Cambodia.

SNIFF SNIFF, PROCEED WITH CAUTION!

A RAT RACE

Like hamsters, these rats have pouches in their cheeks to store extra food.

Rats aren't usually celebrated as heroes. But when they contribute to the extraordinarily dangerous work of clearing land mines, that's exactly what they are. African giant pouched rats can be trained to sniff out buried land mines or explosives left over from war and other conflicts. But don't worry about their safety; the cat-size rats weigh only about two pounds (1 kg), so they aren't heavy enough to set off any mine they might discover. They scurry across the landscape, searching more than 2,150 square feet (200 sq m) of ground in just 20 minutes. It would take a human all day to search even a quarter of that! The rats are trained to sniff out chemical explosives, like TNT, and when they find them, they stop and scratch at the spot to signal their handlers. These special rats save countless lives, and they also restore land so that people can live and farm on it again. Their reward? Peanuts and bananas. Not bad for a hard day's work!

MINNIE

MIGHTY MINNIE

Minnie was a tiny, young foal seemingly born in the wrong place at the wrong time—except that the men of the Lancashire Fusilier 20th Column in Burma during World War II desperately needed her. Minnie had been born into battle, so she did not fear noise and chaos. She willingly followed her men and carried their loads, and for that, the men loved her even more. When an artillery shell injured Minnie, word spread quickly among the troops. She survived but was too fragile to move north with the men. Orders came down to abandon her, but the soldiers refused. A decision was made: Minnie would not be left in the jungle at the mercy of the enemy. But how to smuggle her to safety? What the men were about to do would break the rules. Minnie would have to be flown out, and a tiny airstrip had to be cleared before a getaway plane could safely land. Officers of all ranks turned blind eyes as arrangements were made and the tiny horse, who had claimed so many hearts, was transported to a base in India, where she lived out her life in safety.

MAS: FOUR-LEGGED LIFEGUARD

He's jumped out of helicopters to save drowning swimmers. He's leaped from speeding boats to haul scared or injured swimmers to safety. It's all in a day's work for some lifeguards ... even four-legged ones like Mas the Newfoundland dog. Mas was the first of what became hundreds of specially trained dogs in Italy's corps of canine lifeguards. These "lifedogs" wear harnesses or tow buoys that victims can grab, or rafts they can sit on. They spend up to three years in training with a human lifeguard, and the pair works as a team. Each summer these dogs help swimmers on Italy's crowded beaches. The Italian Coast Guard says it rescues about 3,000 people a year, and credits its intelligent, loyal K9 lifeguards with saving lives. It's all in a day's work for these wonderdogs!

The Italian School of Water Rescue Dogs (Scuola Italiana Cani Salvataggio) has trained about 300 rescue dogs.

ONE OF MAS'S DESCENDANTS POSES WITH TRAINER FERRUCIO PILANGA.

NONJA'S
MASTERPIECES

NONJA

NONJA'S NEW PERSPECTIVE

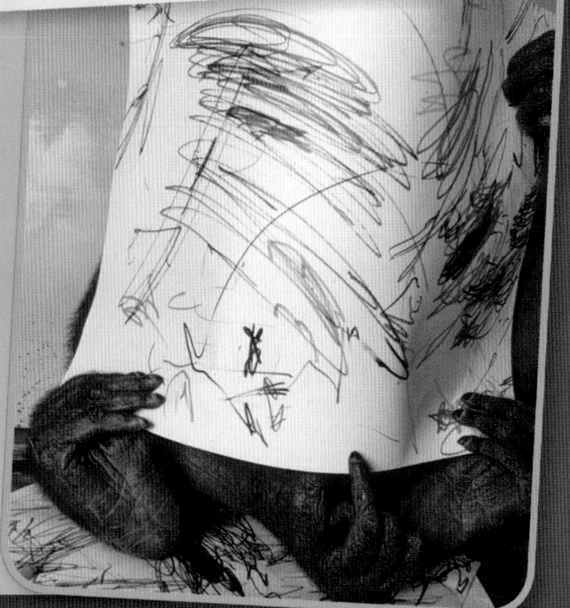

Nonja does her best work in the morning, between 7 and 9, well before any visitors arrive. She doesn't like distractions while she paints. She prefers large canvases, and she uses a thick brush. She usually tastes the paint before applying it. Sound strange? Maybe. But after all, this artist is an orangutan! Nonja lives at the Vienna Zoo in Austria. Nonja may be a talented painter, but she also loves photography. In 2009, the zoo gave her a special, accident-proof camera that released a raisin when a picture was taken—a good incentive for a hungry artist. The camera also had a built-in Wi-Fi connection and automatically uploaded Nonja's photos to her social media page, where thousands of visitors followed her work. Nonja's paintings and photos do what all good artwork should: They inspire. Not bad for an artist who tastes the paint!

RINTY

During the silent movie era, a feature film actor might earn $50 to $100 a week. Rin Tin Tin earned $2,300 a week.

SILENT MOVIE STAR:

RIN TIN TIN

LIGHTS ... CAMERA ... ACTION!

During World War I, Corporal Lee Duncan and his battalion visited a bombed-out war-dog kennel in Lorraine, France. The only survivors were a litter of German shepherd puppies. Duncan became attached to one particular pup, named him Rin Tin Tin, and took him home to California. "Rinty" was a handsome dog—intelligent and athletic. In a true rags-to-riches tale, he began a career as a Hollywood movie star, becoming the highest-earning "actor" for Warner Brothers Studio. Revenue from Rin Tin Tin's films saved the company from bankruptcy. Audiences loved and admired Rinty, and he was often cast in the role of an intelligent hero. Rin Tin Tin received up to 10,000 fan letters a month from all over the country, and was the only dog listed in the Los Angeles telephone directory. But Rin Tin Tin wasn't just living life as a top dog—his popular movies inspired countless people, bringing joy to many who needed it.

ZARAFA

WITH LOVE FROM EGYPT TO PARIS!

ZARAFA

Sometimes it's hard to find the perfect gift. Especially if it's 1826, you're the viceroy of Egypt, and you need an extravagant gift for the king of France! The viceroy asked Egypt's sultan for suggestions. His idea? A giraffe named Zarafa. But how do you get an Egyptian giraffe all the way to France? You send it on a 3,100-mile (5,000-km) trek from what is now southern Sudan to Paris. Zarafa sailed down the Nile and crossed the Mediterranean Sea. Her incredible journey even included being strapped to the back of a camel! And then there was the long walk from Marseille, where Zarafa's ship docked in France. Nevertheless, Zarafa became a star—and the first giraffe to set foot on French soil. In Lyon, almost one-third of the city's population—some 30,000 people—lined the streets to get a glimpse of her. After 41 days of travel, Zarafa at last arrived in Paris. She made her home at the Jardin des Plantes, where she lived for the next 18 years. While there, Zarafa inspired poems, songs, plays, and even a hairstyle! Zarafa had become not just a present for the kings, but a gift to all of France.

VOTE FOR STUBBS!

In 1997, the tiny town of Talkeetna, Alaska, elected a write-in candidate as mayor. But the new mayor, Stubbs, had no real interest in politics. He preferred drinking water and catnip from a margarita glass! Quirky mayoral behavior? Not when the mayor is a cat! As legend has it, Stubbs came to *paw*-ffice after disgruntled townsfolk, unhappy with the field of human candidates, wrote his name on the ballot. And once they had a cat in office, they never went back. Stubbs "served" as town mayor for more than 18 years until his death. Despite lacking any true legislative powers, it is said that his approval rating was the cat's meow.

STUBBS

BLITZ DOGS

Throughout the German Blitz against Britain in 1940 and 1941, Hitler aimed to destroy London and discourage the British population. For 57 consecutive days, London was bombed day and night. Residents sought shelter wherever they could—mostly underground. As more and more homes were hit, people became trapped in the rubble, in need of rescue. Today's search and rescue teams view dogs as essential in their operations, but during World War II, this type of work was in its infancy, with a group of brave dogs rising to the challenge.

"Blitz" means "lightning" in German.

After the war, Peter demonstrated mountain rescue techniques to other rescue dogs and handlers.

PETER

During World War II, the Germans used a flying bomb that the Allies called a Doodlebug. The bombs damaged large areas, creating huge craters. Peter, a collie dog, had been trained to search for wounded people trapped in damaged buildings. He saved many lives. His most triumphant moment came when he rescued a small boy in Chelsea after one of the last Doodlebug attacks on London. But perhaps his most unusual rescue came one evening while he was searching a collapsed house. Peter gave a strong indication to workers that they should dig in a specific area, so they began removing debris. After a short while, a voice could be heard under the soil. The voice sounded upset, and it was saying well, *bad words*. A lot of really bad words! The rescuers worked at a furious pace to release the poor, frightened victim. When the last of the wreckage was removed, they found a large and angry parrot! It was clearly annoyed but otherwise in good health. In 1945, Peter received the Dickin Medal for his wartime service.

PETER WAS A COLLIE LIKE THIS ONE.

 IRMA

An especially gifted rescue dog, Irma the German shepherd had a special bark she used when she detected someone. One of her more remarkable rescues took place in a residential neighborhood. A V-2 rocket had struck during the early morning hours, leveling four homes and badly damaging 12 others. Climbing among the debris, Irma soon sensed something. Human rescuers called for silence so they could listen for any sounds, and that's when they heard a baby crying. A frantic effort began as rescuers clawed at the still smoldering ruins. After two hours of backbreaking digging, infant Paul Raven and his toddler brother were pulled from the wreckage. The boys recovered from their injuries, and in 1950, they reunited with Irma. Said Paul Raven: "We would have lost our lives had it not been for Irma."

IRMA

Irma rescued 191 wounded people trapped under blitzed buildings in London during WWII. She received the Dickin Medal for her service in 1945.

JET

JET

Jet continued his rescue work after the war and played a pivotal role in an operation at the site of a collapsed mine in Whitehaven, England, in 1947. Jet alerted rescuers to an unstable section of the mine, and his warning saved their lives.

Like Irma, Jet the German shepherd served as a search-and-rescue dog during the Blitz. He was credited with saving more than 50 lives! One incredible rescue came at the site of a bombed-out hotel where many people were known to be trapped belowground. After a 12-hour shift, Jet left the spot where rescuers were digging and indicated another place—aboveground—they should look. The rescuers thought Jet might be confused, but he refused to stand down. He even tried to scale a mountain of burning debris to reach the victim he knew to be there. Rescuers brought in ladders and climbed to what was left of an upper floor. They discovered a 63-year-old injured woman, who went to a hospital and made a full recovery. Jet received the Dickin Medal in 1945 for his tenacity and dedication to his work.

ROCKY THE PARACHUTING *WHAT?*

ROCKY WAS AN ASIAN BLACK BEAR LIKE THE ONE PICTURED HERE.

Close your eyes and picture it: a parachuting bear. And a patriotic one at that! During the Korean War in the early 1950s, the American men of AAA battery of the 187th Airborne Regimental Combat Team wanted a mascot. They purchased Rocky, an Asian black bear cub, for about 40,000 yen (about U.S. $111) from a zoo in Japan. But during her "tour of duty," Rocky became much more than a mascot to her brothers in arms. She fought alongside them, taking part in five parachute jumps—one assisted and four on her own. She served with distinction, largely by terrifying the enemy who did not expect to see a bear on the battlefield! Rocky earned a Purple Heart after coming under enemy fire and being injured by shell fragments. Like many animals of war, Rocky's efforts in the conflict were thrust upon her. But despite the fact that she had no choice in the matter, Rocky displayed a loyalty and ability to work with humans that amazed and inspired people. Before the conflict ended, the men in Rocky's unit raised $500 to send her stateside to safety. Rocky found a new home at Lincoln Park Zoo in Chicago, Illinois, where her loyalty and bravery were celebrated.

Her five jumps officially qualified Rocky as a paratrooper.

PELORUS JACK

JACK WAS A RISSO'S DOLPHIN LIKE THE ONE SEEN HERE.

The crew of the ship *Brindle* nervously eyed the channel. To reach Wellington, New Zealand, they had to squeeze through a small and notoriously dangerous waterway with rocks and strong currents. The captain held his breath. Suddenly, a head popped out of the water—it was a Risso's dolphin! The dolphin swam directly in front of the ship, guiding them safely through the channel. After that 1888 incident, that same dolphin, Pelorus Jack, guided all the ships that plowed through that pass. But in 1904, a mean-spirited passenger on one of the boats tried to shoot Jack! The man was quickly wrestled to the deck and locked up. There was little the law could do, however. There was no legal protection for dolphins. That's when the governor, Lord Plunket, signed an order that made it illegal for anyone to harm Jack. New Zealand became the only country to have a special provision for the protection of a single marine creature. Pelorus Jack could safely continue his work! Jack continued to guide ships through the pass for 24 years after first meeting the *Brindle*, until he passed away at a ripe old age for a seafaring scout.

Risso's dolphins are usually found offshore in deep waters.

HELLO, DOLLY

Dolly seemed like an ordinary sheep. She ate grass, she bleated and *baa*-ed; she did everything else regular sheep do. But Dolly was anything but ordinary. She was the first of her kind. Well ... technically, she was the *second:* Dolly was a clone. Researchers at the Roslin Institute in Scotland had been working on cloning, and they thought the key to success might be stem cells, which are cells that can turn into other types of cells. Dolly was the first mammal to be cloned from an adult stem cell. Not only was she a fine sheep, but in creating her, scientists also learned important information. Because of Dolly, new treatments for certain diseases, such as Parkinson's disease or multiple sclerosis, could be developed. During her long life, Dolly wasn't aware of her impact on cloning research. She just focused on eating grass, like the rest of the sheep. But we will never forget her *woolly* fantastic contribution.

Dolly was the only lamb born from 277 attempts.

DOLLY

RIFLEMAN KHAN

Lance Corporal James Muldoon of the 6th Cameronians named his German shepherd Rifleman Khan. Together, they fought in World War II battles across Western Europe. Trained to find explosives, Khan is best known for his brave actions one night in Belgium. Ports along a land bridge called the Walcheren Causeway had to be cleared of Germans to supply Allied troops on mainland Europe. Muldoon and Khan's landing craft came under heavy fire during a night attack and capsized. Khan made for the shore, but he turned back to search for his master. Muldoon couldn't swim. His heavy pack was pulling him under the cold black water. Khan didn't hesitate. He dove back into the water and rescued Muldoon, dragging him ashore under enemy sniper fire. They both survived, and Khan received the Dickin Medal in 1945 for his heroism.

I AM A GOOD DOG!

RIFLEMAN KHAN

A DINOSAUR NAMED SUE

Fossil hunter Susan Hendrickson worked for a company that had been searching for dinosaur bones in the hot, dry hills of South Dakota. On this day in 1990, though, she was just out for a walk with her dog. But as she walked along the base of some cliffs, she spotted two pieces of dark brown bone on the ground. She looked up at the cliffs to see where they might have come from only to see more bones sticking straight out of the cliff face! These bones were larger. *Much* larger. It took six people 17 days to free the dinosaur from the rocks. Susan had discovered the skeleton of the largest, most complete, and best-preserved *Tyrannosaurus rex* in the world, which was quickly named "Sue," in her honor. Sue the dinosaur even had a wishbone and ear bone—two *T. rex* bones archaeologists had never seen before. Sue's discovery allowed scientists to know more than ever before about the *T. rex!*

Sue's skeleton weighs 3,922 pounds (1,779 kg)—the skull alone weighs 600 pounds (272 kg)! In life, the dinosaur probably weighed more than nine tons (8.2 t).

SUE

READY FOR TAKEOFF!

Traveling by air can be a stressful experience. But the San Francisco International Airport tries to reduce any stress by turning to a surprising helper: a therapy pig! Although many airports enlist therapy dogs to greet passengers and reduce anxiety, San Francisco's pig is unique. Named LiLou, she's the first pig to be certified in the Animal Assisted Therapy Program of the San Francisco Society for the Prevention of Cruelty to Animals. LiLou's presence, as well as the pink tutu and pilot's hat she wears, relax anxious travelers. She also performs a few tricks to charm flyers: She can greet you with her snout or hoof, twirl on her back hooves, and even play a toy piano. LiLou devotes herself to putting smiles on passengers' faces and helps make what could be a stressful day easier.

LiLou

HAM: ASTRO CHIMP

UP, UP, AND BEYOND!

HAM

They say that breakfast is the most important meal of the day. That's why on the morning of January 31, 1961, Ham began with a healthy meal of baby cereal, condensed milk, some vitamins, and half an egg. Sufficiently fortified, Ham was then helped into his Redstone rocket and shot into space. Ham was on an important mission to prove that animals in space could carry out tasks during launch, weightlessness, and reentry to earth's atmosphere. Ham was just the man—er, chimpanzee—for the job. He had been trained to pull levers in response to flashing lights for banana pellet rewards. Easy-peasy. And Ham carried out this task while traveling at 5,000 miles an hour (8,000 km/h) more than 155 miles (250 km) above Earth! He was even weightless for about six and a half minutes. Ham's flight intensified an already stiff competition between the United States and the Soviet Union to be first into space. At least one American was truly grateful to Ham—because of his mission's success, astronaut Alan Shepard became America's first human in suborbital flight on May 5, 1961. Hopefully he had a good breakfast as well!

HAM IN HIS "FLIGHT-COUCH."

UNLATCH COVER WHEN NOT IN USE

SEABISCUIT:
THE PEOPLE'S CHAMPION

SEABISCUIT

"The Biscuit" was named Horse of the Year in 1938. When his 89-race career ended, he was the all-time leading earner with $437,730.

During the Great Depression, when many faced tough times, people found an unlikely champion and symbol of hope in a horse named Seabiscuit. Though bred for racing, Seabiscuit was small and knobby-kneed, and he seemed too laid-back to be a winner. His racing career began badly—he lost his first 17 races, usually finishing at the back of the field. But when trainer Tom Smith laid eyes on Seabiscuit in 1936, he knew the horse could be a champion. Seabiscuit just needed training. Smith and jockey Red Pollard had their work cut out for them, but against the odds, Seabiscuit began to win. Soon, this scrappy horse began beating the best racehorses in the country. In 1937, he won 11 of his 15 starts, and won the most money of any horse. Seabiscuit's unbridled spirit and come-from-behind story made him a celebrity and hero to millions.

A sea biscuit is a type of cracker eaten by sailors and is a synonym for hardtack. Hard Tack was the name of Seabiscuit's father.

SIMON: BATTLE CAT

Many cats don't like water, but Simon didn't seem to mind it much—after all, he was a ship's cat! Simon served aboard the British warship H.M.S. *Amethyst*. In 1949, the *Amethyst* steamed up the Yangtze River to Nanjing, China on its way to protect the British Embassy. But the ship didn't get far before it fell into an ambush. Under heavy fire, poor Simon was seriously wounded. No one expected him to survive his injuries. But not only did he recover, he went on to help save his shipmates. The *Amethyst* had beached on a sandbar and found itself surrounded by an enemy that planned to starve out the British. Before long, hordes of rats made their way onto the ship, attacking its dwindling food supply. That's when Simon's feline hunting instincts kicked in. He flew into action! With each rat he caught, he raised the demoralized crew's spirits. They survived the three-month siege thanks in part to Simon's efforts.

For his devotion to duty despite suffering terrible injuries, Simon received the PDSA Dickin Medal. He's the only cat to have received it.

SIMON

ANGEL'S STORY

Angel was found in South Central Los Angeles with chemical burns down her back, puncture wounds on her legs, and mutilated ears. The shelter staff had, sadly, seen these kinds of injuries before. They are especially common on pit bull–type dogs, who are often used for forced breeding and fighting. At the shelter, Angel was initially labeled a "leave alone" dog because the staff thought she might not do well with humans. But they soon learned that despite the trauma she'd endured, Angel just wanted to give and receive love—and kisses! Her spirit remained unbroken. Luckily, actress and comedian Rebecca Corry adopted Angel, changing the trajectory of her life. Angel's story inspired Corry to establish the Stand Up for Pits Foundation, dedicated to saving lives and ending abuse and discrimination of "pit bull–type dogs" (often affectionately called pibbles). In March 2014, Corry and Angel led the One Million Pibble March on Washington, D.C., to raise awareness. Although the world had shown cruelty to Angel, she became—and remains—an inspiration.

ANGEL

MARY OF EXETER:
"THE BIRD WHO WOULD NOT GIVE UP"

MARY

Even against the high standards upheld by every carrier pigeon, Mary of Exeter stands out for her bravery and dedication. By 1940, when British agents dropped Mary of Exeter behind enemy lines in France during World War II, the Germans had started training hawks to intercept pigeons. Being a messenger was more dangerous than ever. Mary survived an attack on her first mission with a deep wound from her neck to her breast. But she delivered her message, recovered, and returned to active duty. Incredibly, just two months later, Mary was shot three times by the German Army, yet still successfully completed her mission. Again, she recovered and returned to duty—only to be wounded again, so severely that people thought she might not survive. But Mary never gave up! She received the Dickin Medal for her outstanding bravery. Of all the courageous animals to receive the award, Mary's resilience and determination remain unmatched and inspiring. She always delivered her message—no matter what.

SALTY:
GUIDING EYES

On September 11, 2001, when terrorists hijacked four airplanes and carried out attacks in the United States, Salty and his owner, Omar Rivera, found themselves on the 71st floor in Tower 1 of New York City's World Trade Center. Rivera is blind but smelled smoke and felt the building sway. He knew they needed to get out of the building. But how? Salty, Rivera's guide dog, helped Rivera to the stairs along with Rivera's supervisor. About halfway down the chaotic and crowded stairwell, Rivera began to despair. He said: "The noise and the heat were terrible. I had to give Salty a chance to escape." He unclipped Salty from his leash. But Salty refused to abandon Rivera. He'd been quickly separated from Rivera when he was unleashed, so he turned and fought his way back *up*, heading toward danger. He found Rivera and took up his position by his side, guiding him all the way down the stairs to safety. Salty's extreme love and loyalty saved Rivera that day.

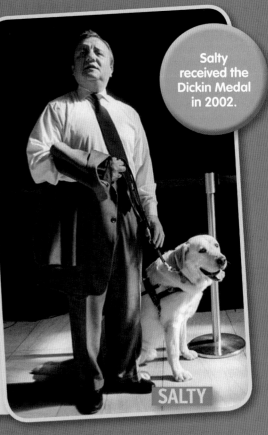

Salty received the Dickin Medal in 2002.

SALTY

Wolf litters average three to six pups.

THE SAWTOOTH PACK

What would it be like to have wolves for neighbors? For six years, wildlife filmmakers Jim and Jamie Dutcher learned the answer to that question by living with a pack of wolves at the edge of Idaho's Sawtooth Wilderness. The pack showed the Dutchers how wolves hunt, play, and raise their young. But one larger lesson stood out: A wolf pack is a family. At the head of this particular family was Kamots, the alpha male. He was the leader of the pack, responsible for the welfare of all the wolves. Then there was Matsi, the beta wolf. Second in command to Kamots, Matsi was the peacekeeper and the pupsitter. Lakota, Kamots's brother, was the omega, or lowest-ranking wolf. Lakota often faced teasing and always ate last. But the omega also fills the key role of class clown, helping ease tensions in the pack, and acting as the glue that keeps the pack together. Together, these wolves formed part of a family—one like any you might find in the human world! Much of the Dutchers' groundbreaking research of Kamots's pack became the foundation for what we know about wolves today.

KAMOTS

AMAZING APES

Scientists have long known that humans and other great apes are closely related. But just what does this connection mean? These amazing gorillas not only learned to communicate directly with humans—they also taught us invaluable lessons.

MICHAEL

KOKO

Both Koko and Michael used the sign "stink" for "flowers," "drink" for "water," and "lip" for "girl."

MICHAEL PUIG

Michael Puig's best teacher sometimes lost patience with him. In fact, she often called him "toilet devil," which is a pretty bad insult—especially when it comes from a gorilla! Michael was an orphaned silverback gorilla who, when he was three years old, came to live with Koko, a western lowland gorilla who communicated using modified American Sign Language. With help from researcher Francine "Penny" Patterson and Koko, Michael learned more than 600 signs! In addition to all that signing, he became an accomplished artist. He painted many abstract scenes with elaborate stories behind them, which he liked to tell his friends.

MICHAEL

ALL BALL

CONVERSATIONS WITH KOKO

Koko and Francine "Penny" Patterson were having a conversation one day. They were using modified American Sign Language because Koko didn't speak. Koko was, in fact, a gorilla! Penny asked Koko what she wanted for Christmas. "Cat!" she signed. Koko wanted a pet! So Koko got a tailless kitten, whom she named "All Ball." A gorilla having a pet cat might seem unusual, but Penny was used to Koko being exceptional. As a Ph.D. student at Stanford University, Penny's research project—to teach sign language to a gorilla—was supposed to last four or five months. Instead the two were together more than 45 years. Koko learned more than 1,000 words—a vocabulary comparable to that of a three-year-old human child—and could understand around 2,000 spoken English words. She not only grasped basics, she also understood emotions and abstract concepts. Koko's accomplishments weren't just a big deal for her; they changed the world's thinking about animal intelligence.

PENNY DIRTY TOILET DEVIL.

KOKO

Koko invented phrases of her own, and some of them were insults! Once, when she was upset, Koko signed her worst insult: "Penny dirty toilet devil."

DIGIT

GORILLAS IN HER MIDST

Dian Fossey didn't really know anything about mountain gorillas when she set up camp on the slopes of the 14,000-foot (4,267-m) Virunga Volcanoes of Rwanda in 1967. Even so, Fossey devoted the following 14 years to living in the harsh climate of a foreign country to learn about these shy animals. She discovered that gorillas lived peacefully, but had many enemies in the form of poachers. Fossey may have learned the most from a gorilla named Digit, whom she first met when he was only a few years old. He was a playful and curious youngster, and grew into a trusting, gentle adult. But one day, poachers killed Digit, who had sacrificed himself so the rest of his group could escape. The loss devastated Fossey. Eventually, she turned her grief into activism and established a fund for antipoaching efforts. Fossey is credited with changing the public's perception of gorillas. Because of her conservation work, mountain gorillas are the only apes with an increasing population, ensuring that Digit's legacy continues.

Fossey learned that mountain gorillas have families, like humans, and are largely vegetarian.

Digit was named for a damaged finger on his right hand.

CHASER: GENIUS DOG

People say elephants have excellent memories, but it's Chaser the border collie who has the largest tested memory of any nonhuman animal. She has more toys than most dogs could dream of, but she can identify and retrieve 1,022 toys by name and by category! Retired professor and psychologist Dr. John W. Pilley trains Chaser five hours a day, five days a week, helping her learn new words and practicing her skills. Don't worry, it's not all work for Chaser; she gets plenty of play and praise. Her toy collection includes 800 cloth animals, 116 plastic balls, and more than 100 plastic toys—each with a unique name. Pilley also taught this precocious pooch that nouns and verbs have different meanings. He can tell Chaser to "paw" a toy, "nose" it, or "take" it, and she will know what to do. Scientists don't yet know what to make of Chaser's skill and intelligence, but she's shown them—and the world—just what dogs are capable of.

Here are the names of only a few of Chaser's toys: Bamboozle, Chuckit, Ernie the Worm, Giggly Wiggly, I-Wanna, Mammy, Oink, Porkchop, Swing Zocker, Tadpole, Uncle Fuzz, and—of course—Woof!

CHASER

A FUNERAL FOR A FLY

The lavish funeral was not to be missed. *Anyone* who was anyone was there. Sad songs were sung. Speeches were given. Professional mourners ... well, *mourned*. Who had died? It was the "pet" fly of Virgil, the famous Roman Empire poet. Wait, what? That's right—legend has it that an extravagant ceremony for a dead fly was held at Virgil's estate. But it was actually a clever ruse to protect Virgil's property. At the time, a battle for power had taken place in Rome. The winning party decided to take the estates of the rich and turn them over to war veterans. Only one exception was given: If the estate held a burial plot, it could not be touched. Supposedly, when Virgil heard that, he hatched his plan. No one was buried on his land, so he staged the elaborate funeral for a dead fly. Virgil's fly was laid to rest in a special tomb on the estate. By burying it, Virgil saved his home. He was able to stay, and eventually completed one of the most famous poems of all time—the *Aeneid*—thanks to a fly!

The cost of the fly's funeral would have been about $1.6 million in today's currency!

VIRGIL

AT WAR WITH PRIVATE WOJTEK

Wojtek, a Syrian brown bear, had been orphaned in spring 1942 in the mountains of Persia. He was discovered by the 22nd Transport Company, Artillery Division, Polish 2nd Corp. The group happily adopted Wojtek as their mascot, but the men had no way of knowing that Wojtek would one day serve alongside them. The following year, the 22nd took part in one of the longest and most brutal battles in Italy during World War II. Their task was to break through German defenses at Monte Cassino near Rome. During the conflict, Wojtek found himself at the artillery firing line. He saw soldiers unloading 25-pound (11-kg) artillery shells from trucks and passing them hand to hand to the front lines. To the shock of many, Wojtek joined right in, carrying artillery shells up to the front.

Within a week, the 22nd delivered 17,320 tons of ammunition, 1,200 tons of fuel, and 1,116 tons of food to the front-line troops. The soldiers' efforts—human and bear alike—helped assure a German defeat.

Animals were not permitted to accompany the army during the fighting, so Wojtek's company had him officially enlist! With his own paybook, rank, and serial number, no one could question whether he was part of the unit. And no one did.

PRIVATE WOJTEK

GALLIPOLI MURPHY

MURPHY

The Battle of Gallipoli during World War I featured many heroes—including some unexpected ones. John Simpson Kirkpatrick of the 3rd Field Ambulance of the Australian Army Medical Corps was at Gallipoli, along with his donkey, Murphy. A donkey may seem like an unusual presence on a battlefield, but Murphy turned out to be remarkably useful. He could carry heavy ammunition to the front lines and bring water to the troops. Perhaps most importantly, a donkey like Murphy could rescue the injured. With both sides trapped by enemy fire, Kirkpatrick and Murphy began trekking back and forth to the front line to retrieve or give aid to the wounded. The route took them straight through deadly sniper and shrapnel fire each time. Despite the risk, Murphy moved slowly and purposefully so as to not add to any injured soldier's pain. Countless lives were saved by this man and his simple and heroic ... donkey.

It was said that if Gallipoli Murphy swished his ear, take cover! He seemed able to detect when a particularly lethal type of shell was about to hit.

LIBRARY CAT

When librarian Vicki Myron heard purring inside the Spencer Public Library's drop box, she was more than a little surprised. It turned out that someone had slipped an eight-week-old kitten in the slot one January night. Winter nights can be brutal in Iowa, U.S.A., and the poor kitten was curled into a frightened, frozen ball. Spencer was a small farming community that had been hit hard by economic troubles in the late 1980s. Myron figured someone who couldn't afford to feed a cat hoped the library could help. So just like that, the library got a pet. Word spread fast, and soon regular and first-time visitors filled the building to see the *purr*-fect addition. The townsfolk even took to calling their library cat Dewey. Sometimes Dewey could be naughty; he might steal a patron's seat, or nap on top of the copier. But the people of Spencer didn't mind. They could identify with this cat: He had come from hard beginnings, just like them. And he was a survivor, just like them. Dewey brought joy and hope to a town that needed it.

Dewey was named after Melvil Dewey, inventor of the Dewey decimal library classification system.

DEWEY

FREEING KEIKO

Ever think an orca could be a movie star? It happened to Keiko, star of the movie *Free Willy*. Movie scouts "discovered" him in Mexico City. He was living in poor conditions at an amusement park. *Free Willy* became a worldwide success, and a lot of moviegoers wanted to know what would happen to Keiko afterward. A public letter-writing campaign to get him released from captivity began. Reintegrating Keiko with a pod of wild orcas would cost more than $20 million and, even more challenging, nothing like it had ever been done before. Eventually, Keiko moved to a state-of-the-art rescue and rehabilitation facility at the Oregon Coast Aquarium in Newport, Oregon. Then, eventually, he was flown to his home waters of Iceland. In 2002, Keiko was released into the open Atlantic. Not everyone considered Keiko's story a success; he had trouble rejoining wild pods and lived out his days near human villages. However, thanks to the inspiring "Free Keiko" movement, many people learned about the challenges and costs of holding marine life captive. It was the beginning of a long journey toward improved treatment for whales and dolphins.

KEIKO IS LOADED INTO A SPECIAL TRANSPORT TANK.

KEIKO

Keiko means "lucky one" or "blessed child" in Japanese.

George was about five feet (1.5 m) long and weighed nearly 200 pounds (90 kg).

LONESOME GEORGE

No one had seen a Pinta Island tortoise since 1906. To most in the scientific community, it was considered fact that they were extinct. But in 1971, a scientist studying snails couldn't believe his eyes when he saw one of the slow-moving reptiles! The little island in the Galápagos—a volcanic archipelago off the coast of Ecuador—did indeed contain one solitary Pinta Island tortoise. Dubbed Lonesome George from that moment on, he was believed to be the last of his kind and one of the rarest creatures in the world. He became a conservation icon and a shelled celebrity. As the last of his species, George may have been "lonely," but he lived a good life. He was relocated to the Tortoise Breeding and Rearing Center on Santa Cruz Island, where he lived for the next 40 years. When he died—at the estimated age of 100—it marked the end of his species. Or so we thought! Scientists have discovered at least 17 tortoises on the Galápagos Islands that have similar genetic traits to George, including some that may be related to his species. George may not have been the last!

Lonesome George's shell was a "saddleback." It dipped slightly near the front, making it look like a saddle.

LIGHTING
THE WAY

War is a dark time for everyone. More than 16 million people perished during World War I, and many who survived it made sacrifices and suffered hardships. No one's life was left untouched, it seemed. But one unlikely nonhuman contribution brought a ray of hope to soldiers far from home: the humble *Lampyris noctiluca*—commonly known as the European glowworm. Huddled night after night in cold, dark trenches, soldiers couldn't risk exposing themselves to the enemy by using a bright lamp or by lighting a fire. But glowworms emit light through bioluminescence. They're a light source! Enlisted men and officers alike collected the worms by the hundreds in bottles and jars. The worms provided enough faint light to read by, allowing soldiers to pore over intelligence reports, study battle maps, or just read comforting letters from home. Best of all, they had a ray of light when one was sorely needed.

Just 10 glowworms can provide the same amount of illumination as a modern-day roadway light.

BIRDS IN SPACE!

March 22, 1990, was a big day for Earthlings. Hundreds of miles above our planet, there was a birth! After 17 days of incubation, a quail chick hatched in space. And then another, and another. In total, eight quail chicks hatched aboard the Russian space station Mir. Immediately, the chicks became famous throughout the world. They were the first vertebrates from Earth to be born in space. Although the world was obviously excited, the chicks themselves were a little dizzy. As birds, learning to fly is hard enough. Try learning to fly when there's no gravity! The chicks gave it their best, flapping their wings with great effort. But controlling which direction they moved in was something of a mystery. The human cosmonauts aboard Mir soon grew accustomed to seeing quail chicks floating through the capsule at random. Whose idea was this anyway? Don't tell the birds, but Russian scientists thought that quails might be a good food source on long flights! These little birdies did not end up as anyone's supper, but they did teach us a lot about living—and flying—in space.

N° 28   29·IV·95
1725

ROCKY

ROCKY AND ROSDAS: WILDLIFE RANGERS

In October 2014, poachers killed an African elephant in Tarangire National Park in Tanzania. Park rangers Rocky and Rosdus were on the trail, hunting for the killers. First, they visited the scene of the crime. Then they started sniffing for clues—*literally*. Rocky and Rosdus are German shepherds! The dogs have been trained to follow a scent for hours, over all types of terrain—dense brush, wetlands, mountains. They work through heat, heavy rain, and other extreme conditions. It didn't take long for the dogs to pick up the scent of the poachers from their footprints. After five hours, the dogs led their team of human rangers to a house in a small town. Inside, a man admitted that the poachers had stopped there. He gave the rangers the information they needed to make an arrest. Tracker dogs like Rocky and Rosdus send a clear message to poachers: If you hunt elephants, we will hunt you!

YOU BE GOOD, SEE YOU TOMORROW. I LOVE YOU.

ALEX'S
MIGHTY BIRD BRAIN

ALEX

African gray parrots' brains are the size of a walnut.

Alex made up his own word for apple. He called it a "banerry," a combination of the words "banana" and "cherry."

Irene Pepperberg couldn't have known what would happen when she walked into that pet store in Indiana. But she was about to begin a 30-year relationship that would change her life. Pepperberg, a scientist who studied the way animals learn, met Alex, an African gray parrot, that fateful day. After she brought Alex home, she wanted to teach him a few words. But over time, she taught him quite a lot. Alex's vocabulary grew to more than 100 English words! And he wasn't shy about asking for his favorite treat: "Want nut!" Alex could also describe objects, shapes, and colors; do simple math; and understand basic concepts such as "none," "same/different," "bigger/smaller." Alex died at age 31. His last words to Pepperberg were: "You be good, see you tomorrow. I love you." Alex proved to the world that "birdbrains" are pretty bright after all.

LANGUAGE LEARNER

Kanzi means "treasure" in Swahili.

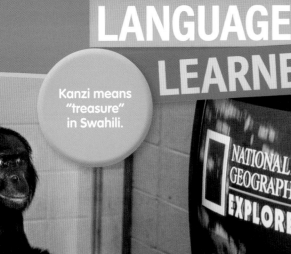

KANZI

Kanzi has a symbol in the lexigram, too:

太

What do you think of when you imagine someone who uses symbols instead of words? A code breaker? A master spy? How about ... a bonobo? Kanzi the bonobo uses lexigrams—symbols that represent words—to communicate. He lives at the Great Ape Trust in Des Moines, Iowa, U.S.A., where, since the 1980s, American psychologist Sue Savage-Rumbaugh and her team have worked with him. Kanzi knows more than 340 symbols and their meanings. He recognizes symbols for familiar objects (yogurt, tummy, bowl), favorite activities (chase, tickle), and even some abstract concepts (now, bad). And if Kanzi can't find the right lexigram to express himself, he'll just create one! When a beaver frightened Kanzi and he didn't have a symbol for the animal, he selected the symbols for "water" and "gorilla" (an animal that scares him) instead. Kanzi can also refer to past and present events and understand others' points of view—skills usually attributed only to humans. But does this ape use language in the same way humans do? Not quite. Studies show that Kanzi is terrible at small talk!

CRIME BUSTER

The sun rose as the Royal Army Veterinary Corps searched a village called Safwan in Iraq in 2003. The soldiers, including a dog named Buster, set about looking for weapons; the village was suspected of hiding terrorists. Tensions ran high, especially because the villagers claimed to be unarmed. The search didn't turn up any weapons at first, but Buster knew otherwise. He entered a house and immediately signaled his handler: Weapons are here! Buster had found a secret stash of weapons hidden in a small cavity inside a wall. Arrests were made, and the village was secured. Buster succeeded where humans had failed, saving civilian and soldier lives through his keen work.

BUSTER

HERO HORSES

Only four horses have received the Dickin Medal since its creation in 1943. The first three were British horses Regal, Olga, and Upstart, who received their awards in recognition of courage exhibited during World War II. All three horses were members of the Metropolitan Police Service. They aided civilians during the German Blitz, a bombing offensive against Britain, and in later bombings from September 1940 to 1944.

REGAL

Most heroic animals gain recognition for something that they *did*. Regal the horse is best known for something he *didn't* do. He never panicked, and his calmness saved the lives of those around him. In one incident, a cluster of bombs struck his stable when no policemen or stable hands were on duty. As the stable burned and flames lapped at Regal, he remained calm, which allowed him to be led to safety. Had he become distressed, he might have endangered the other horses or even the lives of his human rescuers. In another incident, a bomb caused the roof of his stable to collapse on top of him. Regal never got rattled, despite being injured and covered in burning debris. In such an uncertain and unsafe time, many were inspired by Regal's courage and calm.

REGAL

OLGA

Olga was on duty in a British residential town called Tooting during World War II. It had been a quiet, uneventful night when, without warning, a flying bomb called a Doodlebug tore through the town, destroying four houses. Airborne glass sent Olga bolting, but she and her rider quickly steadied themselves and headed into the chaos. They were the first law officers on the scene, and they had a job to do. The four wrecked homes were little more than smoldering piles, and fire was beginning to spread. Injured people needed help. Olga and her rider needed to restore order and prevent panic. They set up a perimeter around the site, controlling traffic to help rescuers reach the injured. Their quick thinking and bravery saved lives that night.

OLGA

UPSTART

Upstart the horse displayed incredible grace under pressure during wartime, even when under direct attack. One night, German bombs struck the London stables where Upstart was housed. Through the smoke and noise of the burning stable, one horse—Upstart—remained calm. He was led to a different stable, only to have it bombed moments later. Upstart escaped the second attack unscathed, but the danger was not over. Not long after, a bomb exploded just 75 feet (23 m) away from the horse and his rider, who were out on patrol. Shards of glass and brick rained down, but when his rider directed Upstart toward the blast, he responded immediately. Together, they helped direct traffic and control the panicked crowd. Upstart's calmness under fire helped keep order and save lives.

UPSTART

UNDERCOVER KITTY

FRED

You might say Fred was unlucky. At least, he certainly had a rough start. When animal control plucked this four-month-old orphaned kitty from the streets of New York, U.S.A., he was dying of pneumonia. But then his luck changed—Fred's health improved and a Brooklyn deputy district attorney who oversaw animal cruelty cases adopted him. It wasn't long before the district attorney's office needed Fred's help. The detectives were investigating a man suspected of acting as a veterinarian without a proper license or training. They had a big job for Fred: He would need to go undercover, posing as a would-be patient. Working with a human detective, Fred was the "bait" in a trap. He did his job perfectly, and the ruse worked! Detectives brought charges against the fake vet. Who knew that a little orphaned cat could help keep countless pets and their owners safer?

JIM THE WONDER DOG

He was runt of the litter and didn't show much promise as a hunting dog. His owner, Missourian Sam Van Arsdale, thought that Jim just wasn't interested. One day during a hunt, Sam told Jim to take a break and sit under the nearby hickory tree. So, he did. There were many trees around, but Jim followed the specific instructions and went directly to the only hickory tree. When Sam named other trees, Jim went straight to those as well. It appeared that Jim had special talents! He could find a specific car by its make, color, or license plate. He could pick people out in a crowd, whether or not he knew them. Jim also seemed able to predict the future, like the time he selected the winner of the 1936 World Series. The country was in a deep economic depression at the time, and money and jobs were scarce. People needed cheering up, which is exactly what this special dog did. Jim the Wonder Dog filled people with wonder—and hope!

Jim also predicted the winner of seven consecutive Kentucky Derbys. He once even predicted that a pregnant cat would give birth to seven kittens, which she did!

JIM

AN ARTIST'S TOUCH

Artists often hear the advice, "Stick with what you know." So, Xiao Qiang mostly sticks to painting watercolor seascapes. Which makes sense because he's a beluga whale! Xiao Qiang is one of Qingdao Polar Ocean World's top attractions in China. He became famous for the incredible aquatic stunts he performs at the aquarium, but now he's known for something else: his art. When a visitor left a paintbrush behind and Xiao Qiang picked it up and began to play with it, his painting career took off. His trainer, Zhang Yong, wondered what would happen if he gave Xiao Qiang some paint. The results were impressive! Xiao Qiang's process involves sticking his head out of the water and holding a paint-filled brush in his mouth. A human assistant holds the paper that Xiao Qiang paints. No wonder Xiao Qiang has such a large following. His art inspires!

XIAO QIANG

I PREFER WATERCOLORS.

ZOND 5
TORTOISES

THE ZOND 5 ASTRONAUTS WERE TORTOISES LIKE THIS ONE.

They looked like ordinary tortoises—kind of small with lumpy brown shells. Nothing special, it seemed. But when the Soviet Union launched them into space on the Zond 5 spacecraft on September 15, 1968, they became remarkable. These tortoises went where no man had gone before! They became the first animals in *deep space* and the first inhabitants of Earth to go around the moon. Their spacecraft made a wide slingshot around the moon, traveling about 1,200 miles (1,931 km) from the surface. Success! They circled the moon. Landing back on Earth was problematic, though. A sensor on the ship failed, ending hopes of a guided reentry. The capsule had a fast and hard landing in the Indian Ocean, and rescuers raced to recover the crew. The tortoises were alive, but very hungry. They had not eaten since before they left! The hero tortoises were quickly fattened up by their grateful nation.

SHEILA: RESCUE READY

On December 16, 1944, a Boeing B-17 Flying Fortress from the U.S. Eighth Air Force crashed on the border between England and Scotland. Two local shepherds headed up the mountainside with their sheepdog, Sheila, to investigate. The men could see nothing—an ongoing blizzard reduced visibility to almost zero. Sheila relied on her other strong senses and set to work, easily tracking down the aircraft. But its crew remained missing. Sheila continued to search through the blinding snow. At last, she found them. The airmen had crawled into a crevice to escape the weather. Sheila then guided the airmen and the shepherds to a nearby cottage. The downed B-17, which was laden with bombs, exploded just as they reached safety. Sheila received the Dickin Medal in 1945, the first time the medal went to a nonmilitary dog.

SHEILA

MY ROOM WITH A VIEW!

LOLA

CITY DWELLER

PALE MALE

Like all city dwellers, Pale Male had to get used to the hustle and bustle of a booming metropolis. And finding a decent place to live in New York can be brutal! Pale Male tried a tree at first, but crows chased him off. So this red-tailed hawk built a nest at the top of an apartment building on Fifth Avenue near Central Park. Could a wild animal succeed in the city? Yes! He found plenty of prey near his new home, and even a mate. The hawks started a family, surprising bird-watchers and conservationists by their ability to overcome adversity and make a life in the city. Pale Male continues to challenge ideas about urban wildlife—and surprise and delight city dwellers when he swoops through the skies.

Pale Male shared the same apartment building with actress and comedian Mary Tyler Moore.

CHRIS P. BACON:

PIG ON WHEELS

Chris P. loves snacking on Cheerios and grapes.

Chris P. wanted to run and play, just like all the other little piggies. But he was born without the use of his back legs. Unsure of what to do, his owner in Florida, U.S.A., contacted Dr. Len Lucero, a veterinarian. Dr. Len saw something special in this pig. So he adopted him, and gave the piglet a silly name: Chris P. Bacon! Chris P. didn't mind; he had a great life, especially after Dr. Len built him a special cart. This miniature pig-mobile helped Chris P. get around and charmed the people who saw him scooting. Dr. Len loved Chris P.'s spirit, and felt inspired by him. Suspecting that others might, too, Dr. Len arranged for Chris P. to visit children who are experiencing physical or mental disabilities. Chris P.'s great attitude and positive spirit serve as a reminder that anything is possible.

Page 12

THE
TRACKING TRIO

CHANGING THE WORLD

Endal the Lifesaver
Page 53

Space Jellies
Page 52

The animals in this book all changed the world in big and small ways. Are you ready to change the world, too? You can! Remember, even a small act can have a big impact.

Born to Live Free Page 58

Psychic Paul Page 28

Begin by asking yourself what you can do right now, where you are, with what you have. Here are a few ideas:

1. **Volunteer.** Offer your time and talent by volunteering in your community. Ask, *What needs doing?* Then find a related organization that needs your time and energy.

2. **Support a cause.** Find something you are passionate about and fight for it. Write letters about your cause to local politicians, hold fund-raisers, and help raise awareness.

3. **Respect others.** Accept people regardless of differences. Treat others with decency and humanity. Erase prejudices and eliminate labels.

4. **Pay it forward.** Hold a door open for someone. Do a chore for someone else. Buy lunch for a friend. It doesn't take a lot to make someone's day a little bit better!

5. **Adopt from your local shelter.** Looking for a new pet? Most animals in shelters are rescues in need of loving homes. You can give an animal a second chance.

6. **Keep the environment clean.** You can change the world by picking up trash—yes, even other people's litter. Just be sure to ask an adult for supervision and the right supplies.

7. **Help the elderly.** With an adult's permission, visit with an older neighbor and ask if they need any help. You might offer to mow a lawn, water a flower bed, or pick up groceries.

8. **Conserve electricity and water.** Turn off appliances and lights when you're not using them. Be mindful about when the tap is running.

9. **Reach out to the homeless.** Donate food or supplies to the homeless or volunteer to serve food to the homeless.

10. **Lead by example.** Be polite and appreciative of the people around you. Be kind. Believe in the goodness of people and believe in the good of the world around you. **And always remember:** You have the power to change the world.

Smokey Bear Page 12

Index

Index

Credits

FRONT COVER: (Chris P. Bacon the pig), Tom Benitez/Orlando Sentinel/MCT/Newscom; (K-Dog the dolphin), Photographer's Mate 1st Class Brien Aho/U.S. Navy; (Fred the cat), ZUMA Press, Inc./Alamy Stock Photo; (Fiona the hippo), AP/REX/Shutterstock; **SPINE:** (Alex the parrot), John Robert Miller/AP/Shutterstock; **BACK COVER:** (Buttercup the sloth), Suzi Eszterhas/Minden Pictures; (Koko the gorilla), Ronald H. Cohen/National Geographic Image Collection; (Ham the chimpanzee), NASA; (Sergeant Stubby the dog), FOR ALAN/Alamy Stock Photo

INTERIOR: 1, Michelle Curley, courtesy of Cincinnati Zoo and Botanical Garden; 2-3, Dutcher Film Productions; 4 (eagle), Young Kwak/AP/Shutterstock; 4 (cat), Courtesy Gabrielle Hendel; 4 (sloth), Debbie Prediger/Alamy Stock Photo; 4 (pony), Phil Masturzo/Akron Beacon Journal/MCT/Newscom; 5 (pig), Jon Busdeker/Orlando Sentinel/MCT/Tribune Content Agency LLC/Alamy Stock Photo; 5 (orca), Ingrid Visser/Minden Pictures; 5 (gorillas in car), Cohn, Ronald H.; 6, REX/Shutterstock; 7 (UP), Tatyana Danilova; 7 (CTR), Suzi Eszterhas/Minden Pictures; 7 (LO), Yoshikazu Tsuno/AFP/Getty Images; 8-9, Mike Hollist/Associated Newspapers/Shutterstock; 10, REX/Shutterstock; 11 (UP), GRANGER - All rights reserved.; 11 (LO), Eric Isselee/Shutterstock; 12 (UP LE), Jeremy Goss, Courtesy of Big Life Foundation; 12 (LO LE), Jeremy Goss, Courtesy of Big Life Foundation; 12 (UP RT), AP/Shutterstock; 12 (CTR RT), Stock Connection/Shutterstock; 13 (ALL), Young Kwak/AP/Shutterstock; 14 (UP), Eric Isselee/Shutterstock; 14 (LO), akg-images; 15 (UP), Amy Stanford Plymouth Herald/AP/Shutterstock; 15 (LO), John Zich/The LIFE Images Collection/Getty Images; 16 (LE), Bridgeman Images; 16 (UP RT), Look and Learn/Bridgeman Images; 17 (UP), Courtesy Eastern State Penitentiary Historic Site; 17 (LO), Hulton Archive/Getty Images; 18 (UP), PJF Military Collection/Alamy Stock Photo; 18 (LO), PJF Military Collection/Alamy Stock Photo; 19, Photographer's Mate 1st Class Brien Aho/U.S. Navy; 20 (UP LE), Keith Srakocic/AP/Shutterstock; 20 (UP CTR LE), Gene J. Puskar/AP/Shutterstock; 20 (LO), The Asahi Shimbun via Getty Images; 21, Franco Tempesta; 22 (UP), Nigel Paul Monckton/Shutterstock; 22 (LO), Library of Congress Prints and Photographs Division; 23 (UP), Courtesy Crockett Family; 23 (LO), Mary Evans Picture Library; 24 (UP), Alaska Stock Images; 24 (LO), Carrie McLain Museum/AlaskaStock; 25 (UP), Latrobe Valley Express/EPA/Shutterstock; 25 (LO), Courtesy Patricia Peter; 26 (ALL), Suzi Eszterhas/Minden Pictures; 27 (UP), Harry Todd/Fox Photos/Hulton Archive/Getty Images; 27 (LO), ITAR-TASS News Agency/Alamy Stock Photo; 28 (ALL), Roberto Pfeil/AP/Shutterstock; 29 (UP), Albert Pedroza/San Antonio Fire Department; 29 (LO), Richard Olsenius/National Geographic Image Collection; 30-31 (ALL), Mike Forster/Daily Mail/Shutterstock; 32 (UP), Historia/Shutterstock; 32 (LO), Courtesy PDSA; 33 (RT), Daily Mail/Shutterstock; 33 (LO LE & INSET), Art Collection 2/Alamy Stock Photo; 34 (UP), Casey Anderson/Montana Grizzly Encounter; 34 (INSET), Casey Anderson/Montana Grizzly Encounter; 34 (LO), Rick Smith/Grizzly Creek Films; 35 (UP), Susan English/Denver Red Cross/Courtesy Denver Red Cross/ZUMAPRESS.com; 35 (LO), Photo courtesy Smoky War Dog LLC; 36 (ALL), TopFoto/The Image Works; 37 (UP), Maidenform Collection, Archives Center, National Museum of American History, Smithsonian Institution; 37 (pigeon), Paul J. Richards/AFP/Getty Images; 37 (message), The U.S. National Archives and Records Administration; 38 (ALL), NASA; 39 (UP), Kevin Rice/AP/Shutterstock; 39 (LO), Karen Schiely/Akron Beacon Journal/TNS/Newscom; 40 (ALL), Courtesy Gabrielle Hendel; 41 (UP), Van Lawick, HUGO/National Geographic Image Collection; 41 (LO), Bill Clark/Getty Images; 42-43, Digital Beach Media/Shutterstock; 42 (ALL), Digital Beach Media/Shutterstock/Shutterstock; 43 (ALL), Chris O'Meara/AP/Shutterstock; 44 (UP), Eye of Science/Science Source; 44 (LO), PJF Military Collection/Alamy Stock Photo; 45, David Keith Jones/Images of Africa Photobank/Alamy Stock Photo; 46 (UP), Paul T. Erickson/MCT/Newscom; 46 (INSET), AP Photo/The Tri-City Herald, Paul T. Erickson; 46 (LO), Friends of Washoe; 47, Bob Daugherty/AP/Shutterstock; 47 (INSET), Charles Tasnadi/AP/Shutterstock; 48 (UP), Detlev van Ravenswaay/Science Source; 48 (LO), RIA Novosti/Science Source; 49 (UP), Sebastian Janicki/Shutterstock; 49 (CTR), Dominic Hart/NASA; 49 (LO), NASA; 50 (ALL), Arshia Khan; 51 (UP), George Silk/The LIFE Picture Collection/Getty Images; 51 (CTR), AP Photo; 51 (LO), Courtesy PDSA; 52 (Faith cat), Courtesy PDSA; 52 (space shuttle), NASA; 52 (jellyfish), pandemin/istock/Getty Images; 53 (RT), Mike Hollist/Daily Mail/Shutterstock; 53 (CTR LE), John Taylor/Shutterstock; 53 (LO LE), Matt Faber/PA Images/Alamy Stock Photo; 54, Angela Hatke, Courtesy Cincinnati Zoo and Botanical Garden; 55 (UP), John Minchillo/AP/REX/Shutterstock; 55 (LO), Amy LaBarbara, Courtesy of Cincinnati Zoo and Botanical Garden; 56 (monkey), David Osborn/Shutterstock; 56 (King Alexander), Archives Larousse, Paris, France/Bridgeman Images; 56 (cat), cdrin/Shutterstock; 56-57 (H.M.S. *Ark Royal*), Bridgeman Images; 57 (*Bismarck*), akg-images/WHA/World History Archive; 57 (spider), Rod Preston-Mafham/Premaphotos/NPL/Minden Pictures; 58 (Elsa lion), Keystone Pictures USA/Alamy Stock Photo; 58 (Veterok & Ugolyok), SPUTNIK/Alamy Stock Photo; 59 (UP, LO LE), Hanson, Michael/National Geographic Image Collection; 59 (LO RT), Eric Isselee/Shutterstock; 60 (ALL), Taro Yamasaki/The LIFE Images Collection/Getty Images; 61 (laboratory cats), Keystone/Getty Images; 61 (Félicette), TopFoto/The Image Works; 61 (wren), Mary Evans/Natural History Museum; 61 (cat), Rosa Jay/Shutterstock; 62-63 (UP), AP/Shutterstock; 62 (UP), Action Plus Sports Images/Alamy Stock Photo; 62 (LO), Bridgeman Images; 63 (LO), Topical Press Agency/Hulton Archive/Getty Images; 64 (UP), Jeremy Selwyn/Evening Standard/Shutterstock; 64 (LO), Rupert Hartley/Shutterstock; 65 (UP), akg-images/picture-alliance/dpa; 65 (LO), Ondrej Prosicky/Shutterstock; 66-67, Claudio Montesano Casillas/Rex Shutterstock; 66 (ALL), Denis Gray/AP/REX/Shutterstock; 67 (UP), Denis Gray/AP/REX/Shutterstock; 68 (UP LE), The Fusilier Museum, Lancashire; 68 (UP RT), Lori Epstein/National Geographic Image Collection; 68 (LO RT), Lori Epstein/National Geographic Image Collection; 69 (UP), Patrick Aventurier/Gamma-Rapho/Getty Images; 69 (INSET), Patrick Aventurier/Gamma-Rapho/Getty Images; 69 (LO), Patrick Aventurier/Gamma-Rapho/Getty Images; 70 (UP), Globe Photos/ZUMAPRESS.com/Alamy Stock Photo; 70 (LO), Granger.com - All rights reserved; 71 (UP), CCI/Bridgeman Images; 71 (LO), Mark Thiessen/AP/REX/Shutterstock; 72 (UP), PA Wire via ZUMA Press; 72 (LO), Eric Isselee/Shutterstock; 73 (ALL), Courtesy PDSA; 74 (UP), I WALL/Shutterstock; 74 (LO), Wild_and_free_naturephoto/Shutterstock; 75 (ALL), James Fraser/Shutterstock; 76 (UP), Pressteam; 76 (LO), Mark Wilson/Newsmakers/Getty Images; 77 (ALL), Courtesy Tatyana Danilova; 78-79 (ALL), NASA; 80, Jerry Cooke/Sports Illustrated/Getty Images; 80 (INSET), Keystone-France/Gamma-Keystone/Getty Images; 81 (UP), PA Images/Alamy Stock Photo; 81 (LO), Virgil Ocampo, Courtesy Stand Up For Pits Foundation; 82 (UP), Courtesy PDSA; 82 (LO), Justin Lane/The New York Times/Redux Pictures; 83 (UP), Dutcher Film Productions; 83 (CTR LE), Jim and Jamie Dutcher/National Geographic Image Collection; 83 (LO), Jim and Jamie Dutcher/National Geographic Image Collection; 84 (UP), Cohn, Ronald H./Gorilla Foundation; 84 (LO), Zuma Press; 85 (UP LE), Ronald Cohn/Gorilla Foundation; 85 (UP RT), Campbell, Robert I.M./National Geographic Image Collection; 85 (LO), Gorilla Foundation; 86 (ALL), Sebastien Micke/Paris Match/Getty Images; 87 (fly), Dimijana/Shutterstock; 87 (Virgil), Vanni Archive/Art Resource, NYImage; 87 (LO), Magdalena Bujak/Alamy Stock Photo; 88 (UP LE), Mary Evans/Robert Hunt Collection; 88 (CTR RT), Charlie Neibergall/AP/REX/Shutterstock; 88 (LO RT), Charlie Neibergall/AP/REX/Shutterstock; 89, Ingrid Visser/Minden Pictures; 89 (INSET), Dave Nolan/USAF/Hulton Archive/Getty Images; 90-91, Tui De Roy/Minden Pictures; 91 (UP), Arturo de Frias/Alamy Stock Photo; 91 (CTR LE), Tui De Roy/Minden Pictures; 91 (LO), David Hosking/Science Source; 92, Shaun Jeffers/Shutterstock; 92 (INSET), Gallinago_media; 93 (UP LE), SergeiSayan/Shutterstock; 93 (LO LE), Tom Trower/NASA; 93 (LO RT), NASA; 93 (UP RT), Kim McCoy; 94 (UP), Gerald Davis/Shutterstock; 94 (LO), John Robert Miller/AP/Shutterstock; 95 (UP), Mint Images/Shutterstock; 95 (LO), Jim Watson/AFP/Getty Images; 96-97 (ALL), Courtesy PDSA; 98 (UP LE), ZUMA/Alamy Stock Photo; 98 (UP RT), David Handschuh/NY Daily News Archive/Getty Images; 98 (LO), Courtesy Friends of Jim the Wonder Dog Organization; 99 (ALL), Yoshikazu Tsuno/AFP/Getty Images; 100 (UP), SPUTNIK/Alamy Stock Photo; 100 (LO), -V-/Shutterstock; 101 (UP RT), Susan Watts/NY Daily News Archive/Getty Images; 101 (CTR RT), Mario Tama/Getty Images; 101 (LO LE), Courtesy PDSA; 102 (UP), Len Lucero/Sipa USA/Newscom; 102-103 (LO), Tom Benitez/Orlando Sentinel/MCT/Newscom; 103 (UP), Tamara Lush/AP/REX/Shutterstock; 103 (LO), Tom Benitez/MCT/Newscom; 104-105, Jeremy Goss/Big Life Foundation; 106 (UP), Paul Watts/REX/Shutterstock; 106 (LO), pandemin/iStock/Getty Images; 107 (Elsa lion), AF archive/Alamy Stock Photo; 107 (Paul octopus), Roberto Pfeil/AP/REX/Shutterstock; 107 (Smokey Bear), Gordon Wiltsie/National Geographic Image Collection; 112, Karen Schiely/Newscom

Petie the
Therapy Pony
Page 39

NATIONAL GEOGRAPHIC and Yellow Border Design are trademarks of the National Geographic Society, used under license.

Since 1888, the National Geographic Society has funded more than 14,000 research, conservation, education, and storytelling projects around the world. National Geographic Partners distributes a portion of the funds it receives from your purchase to National Geographic Society to support programs including the conservation of animals and their habitats. To learn more, visit natgeo.com/info.

For more information, visit nationalgeographic.com, call 1-877-873-6846, or write to the following address:

National Geographic Partners, LLC
1145 17th Street NW
Washington, DC 20036-4688 U.S.A.

For librarians and teachers:
nationalgeographic.com/books/librarians-and-educators

More for kids from National Geographic: natgeokids.com

National Geographic Kids magazine inspires children to explore their world with fun yet educational articles on animals, science, nature, and more. Using fresh storytelling and amazing photography, *Nat Geo Kids* shows kids ages 6 to 14 the fascinating truth about the world—and why they should care. **natgeo.com/subscribe**

For rights or permissions inquiries, please contact National Geographic Books Subsidiary Rights: bookrights@natgeo.com

Designed by Ashita.Design

Library of Congress Cataloging-in-Publication Data

Names: Maloney, Brenna, author. | National Geographic Kids (Firm), publisher. | National Geographic Society (U.S.)
Title: 125 animals that changed the world/by Brenna Maloney.
Other titles: One hundred and twenty-five animals that changed the world
Description: Washington, DC : National Geographic Kids, [2019] | Audience: Ages 8-12. | Audience: Grades 4 to 6. | Includes index.
Identifiers: LCCN 2018031626| ISBN 9781426332777 (pbk.) | ISBN 9781426332784 (hardcover)
Subjects: LCSH: Pets--Anecdotes--Juvenile literature. | Pets--Miscellanea --Juvenile literature. | Animals--Anecdotes--Juvenile literature. | Animals--Miscellanea--Juvenile literature.
Classification: LCC SF75.5 .M356 2019 | DDC 636.002--dc23
LC record available at https://lccn.loc.gov/2018031626

The publisher would like to thank: Brenna Maloney, author; Roberta Lenarz, project manager; Liz Seramur, photo editor; Paige Towler, project editor; Sanjida Rashid, art director; Lori Epstein, photo director; Jennifer Kelly Geddes, fact-checker; Alix Inchausti, production editor; and Anne LeongSon and Gus Tello, design production assistants.

Printed in China
22/HHC/3